MAKING IT
in high heels 2

MAKING IT
in high heels 2

For Future Leaders and Role Models

Edited by Kimberlee MacDonald

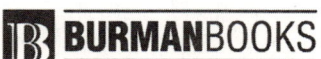
BURMANBOOKS

Copyright © 2009 Making It in High Heels 2

Published by BurmanBooks Inc.
260 Queens Quay West
Suite 904
Toronto, Ontario
Canada M5J 2N3

All rights reserved. No part of this publication may be reproduced, stored in a retrieval system, or transmitted in any form by any process—electronic, photocopying, recording, or otherwise—without the prior written consent of BurmanBooks Inc.

Cover and interior design:
Jack Steiner Graphic Design

Editing:
Kimberlee MacDonald

Distribution:
Trumedia Group
c/o Ingram Publisher Services
14 Ingram Blvd.
LaVergne, TN 37086

ISBN 978-1-897404-07-2

Dedication

To all the women trying their best to make it in this world,
don't give up.
Everyone in this book participated because
they want you to succeed.

Acknowledgments

John the project manager
Bruce for all his legal expertise
Ralph, the wizard of the Net
Jack for all his creativeness in these books
All the girls from the last book who made it such a success

Please visit

www.makingitinhighheels.com

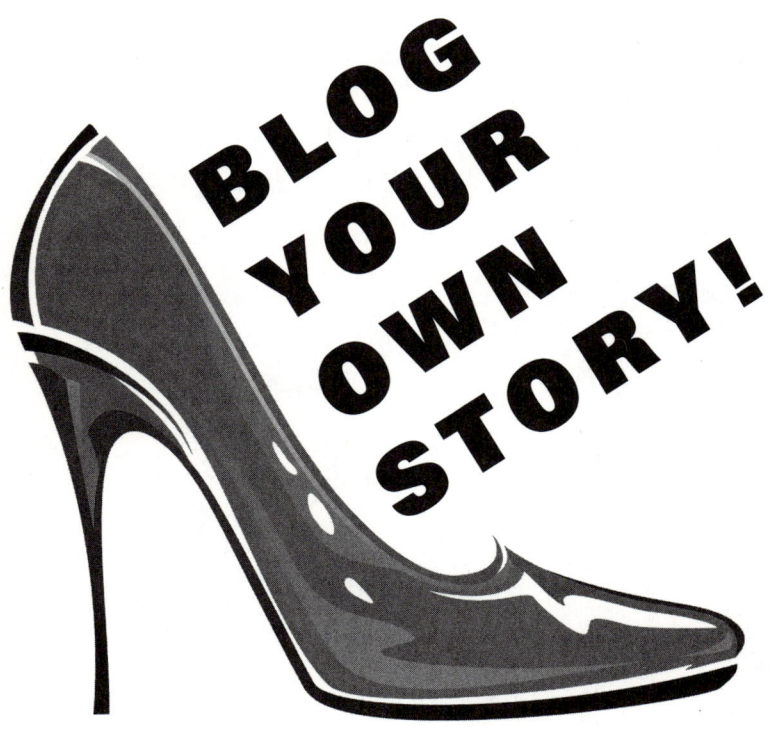

Table of Contents

Ani Chakmakian *1*

Jennifer Snyder *5*

Cheryl Mendes *14*

Daniela Godoy Jameson Cruz *18*

Shelby Way *22*

Ariel Garten *27*

Bianca Gross *33*

Dr. Biljana Durickovic Bsc, DC *40*

Larissa Gomes *47*

Lynn Manwar *57*

Jade Anthony *63*

Elizabeth Grant *72*

Stella Telleria *76*

Tanya Marwah *85*

Lisa Bradburn *89*

Julie Christine *95*

Nirvana Savoury *103*

charysse robinson *112*

Donessa Echols *117*

Bobbie Phillips *126*

Sitara Hewitt *133*

Jacquie Jordan *138*

Kay Ann Ward *141*

Lina Policaro *146*

Katrina Campins *152*

Nimisha Raja *160*

Natascha Trivedi *166*

Karyn Chopik *170*

Roula Papaioannou *178*

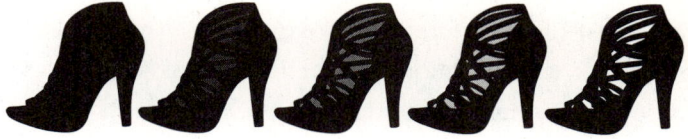

Ani Chakmakian

Before I wanted to make it in high heels, I dreamed of making it on figure skates. For more than ten years, I worked to make my dreams a reality; only to discover that continuing toward my goal would lead to serious health consequences in the future. That sobering reality gave rise to the agonizing decision to leave my dream unrealized. As a teenager, it was painful to let skating go, but the experience opened doors to new possibilities. My story is about overcoming loss and converting your energy and creativity into new and exciting dreams that will enable you to feel fulfilled and empowered. It's about recognizing that losing something you love doesn't mean you can't continue to grow.

I was on skates from the age of two. Like many Canadian girls, I took to the ice with natural ease and soon grew to love everything about skating. The challenging artistry, demanding jumps and beautiful spins were magical. The perfect balance between art and sport and the representation of music in movement made me feel that I had the ability to create something unique and original every time I stepped on the ice. My childhood years were full of the joy that came with doing something I loved. I was so excited to be skating everyday that I was almost always the first one on the ice and the last one to get kicked off by the Zamboni driver. The feel of my blades being the first to etch edges into the fresh, untouched ice was matched only by working to the last minute to perfect a jump before I skated off for the day.

I'd always loved practice. It was my parents and coaches, and later, my teachers, who would tell me to rest. Growing up in Edmonton, I was inspired by the many champion skaters at my rink. Although it was minus 2°C most of the winter, I'd wake up early most mornings and head to the rink with my mom to practice before school started. After class, I'd be back again to skate until dinner. My parents recognized my determination and were always amazingly supportive. I felt lucky that I had the opportunity to learn so much about myself on the ice.

As much as skating was art and sport to me, it was also social education. Early on, I noticed that the other skaters would gather around the boards to chitchat about the jumps the other girls were working on and who would be going to the next competition. One day, when I was eleven, I landed my first double axle. It happened right in the middle of the ice during a very busy summer school session.

I was ecstatic! It was the hardest jump I'd landed yet and no one had asked me to do it; I'd just decided that day would be the day I'd land my axle and I did it. While it was a moment of quiet excitement, it was also a catalyst for spawning animosity from some of the other competitors. I learned from then on how unkind girls can be when they try to measure up to each other, instead of themselves.

Skating is such a demanding sport, not only because of the grueling physical demands, but also because of the psychological challenges. Many young girls find themselves sandwiched between pressures from their parents, their coaches, the sport and their own insecurities. It's hard for some not to take it out on others. Luckily, I skated because I wanted to; because I loved it and later, because I hoped to compete internationally. I had the most supportive parents, the best coaches and support team, with the talent to do what I wanted and the nature to compete with a positive mindset.

I happily and successfully competed until a serious hip injury left me bedridden for a month. I vividly remember experiencing excruciating pain just trying to sit up and watch TV and having to be carried everywhere by my dad. I had dislodged a muscle and ligaments in and around my hip. I remember how concerned the specialists seemed over my X-rays as they discussed a course of treatment, while my anxious parents looked on. I was relieved when I was told that, although I'd have to be very careful, I'd be able to get back on my skates in 12-14 weeks.

Within a few weeks of being back on the ice, however, the same injury occurred again. My injuries had already become chronic and the doctors urged my parents to do the right thing and take me out of skating. They made the decision for me in my best interests; although it took me years to see it that way. It wasn't until I learned that 1998 Olympic Champion *Tara Lipinski* received a double hip replacement at the age of 18 that I understood what the doctors were talking about then.

Life after skating was hard, at first. After losing something that I loved and that was a part of my identity for so many years, I struggled to find meaning in my life without it. As a teenager, I spent some time confused and preoccupied with thinking and writing to make sense of my situation. None of my friends at school had experienced anything like what I'd been through, so it was hard to talk about it with any of my peers.

Eventually, I picked up a racquet and started playing tennis. I began competing after five months of training; to the amazement of my coach. Later on, I played volleyball and basketball on junior high sports teams until I found my ultimate interests in high school. It was there that I started to connect with activities I was passionate about again. I kept myself very busy between my honours and International Baccalaureate classes; becoming involved with creative writing, social justice and public speaking. I worked on the school newspaper and raised awareness about landmines; I attended local and national leadership conferences and engaged in fundraising for many charities. I developed long-lasting relationships with peers and adults and immersed myself fully in learning the skills that would carry me through university and into my career in Public Relations today.

Skating taught me perseverance and how to heal from the past and move on. Through its loss, I discovered a reservoir of internal strength that I could draw on to convert my energy into new and fulfilling dreams with the same level of dedication and excitement. It also crystallized my philosophy that competing is a very personal process; it's not about your opponent as much as it is about meeting and exceeding your goals to reach your personal best each time you are put to the test. This approach has stood me well in business, too. Life is too short to look back in regret on things that could have been when there is so much to inspire you in the present moment. My wish for you is to find your inner light and let it shine!

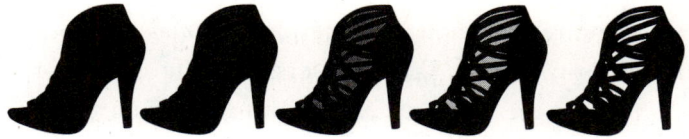

Jennifer Snyder

I believe the athletic foundation upon which I later built was started early. I was riding a motorcycle at the age of five, waterskiing by nine and swimming competitively at twelve. My frame grew quickly; I was a lanky 5'9" by fifth grade and had soared to a lofty 6'2" by my freshman year of high school. My height and athletic ability led me to where I am today; playing professional beach volleyball on the Association of Volleyball Professionals' tour.

During high school, sports seemed to come easily for me. I made the Varsity basketball and Junior Varsity volleyball teams as a freshman. I moved up to Varsity volleyball for Regionals and State at the end of the season. That year, I was also introduced to "club" volleyball. This is the largest girls' sports organization in the country for girls 18 years and under. I began playing club volleyball along with my other high school sports and loved every minute.

Basketball was always my first love and I genuinely believed that I would be going to college on a basketball scholarship. We took Regionals my freshman year and my sophomore year, we were a heavy favorite for the State Championship.

Unfortunately, in December of my sophomore year, at the beginning of both my club volleyball and high school basketball seasons, I ruptured my anterior cruciate ligament (ACL) playing volleyball. I needed total knee reconstruction surgery and would be out for at least nine months; possibly up to a year. I was devastated and so were my teams.

As the basketball season began, I went to practice on crutches everyday to learn the plays and stay in touch with the girls, in case I was healthy enough to return in time for Regionals and State. During one particular practice, I didn't understand one of the plays being taught, so I asked the coach to explain it to me. She replied, "I don't have time right now." I asked if I could come into her office after the practice so she could diagram it for me and she again replied, "I don't have the time, you're just going to have to figure it out on your own time." The coach was so upset with me for getting injured playing club volleyball and ruining her chances for a State Championship that she was unwilling to help me stay prepared for my return. That was the last time I ever played basketball.

On the flip side, my club volleyball coach was in contact with me weekly, came to visit me in the hospital; constantly wanting to know how I was doing and when I would be ready to play again. Leaven Eubank was willing to do anything to help me achieve success and he remains one of my best friends. I have played volleyball ever since.

My volleyball career took off with lightning speed in my junior and senior years. During that time, I was invited to many elite programs, including the Junior Olympic Volleyball team; a developmental program run through USA Volleyball to train and recruit young potential players for the US National Team. I was offered scholarships by many colleges and decided to choose the one that kept me close to home; Arizona State University.

There, I was a loud and arrogant freshman, not seeing any playing time. I felt I was better than I actually was at that point and I voiced my opinions often about how I should be playing instead of the senior year player that was on the court. I'm a little embarrassed when I look back on that time, but I wouldn't change it; it's a part of how I came to be who I am today. In one of the biggest rivalry games during the middle of the season, against the University of Arizona, I was put in the game. I got my chance and never looked back.

I had a great freshman season and was again invited to an elite program put on by USA Volleyball. Olympic Festival is a college level program aimed at grooming young athletes for future national team participation. It was at this event that I first met Kerri Walsh, the future two-time Olympic Gold Medalist for Beach Volleyball. At that time, she was a bright-eyed 16-year-old kid with amazing playing ability. We became friends and a few of us nicknamed her 'Novice.' She was the only high school kid there and she was better than most of us; not surprising, considering her outcome. She remains one of the most amazing people I have ever met. I made many friendships there that I still cherish today. I left with new confidence and a strong desire to further my volleyball opportunities.

At ASU, I played on a team that was talented enough to make it to the round of 16 nationally every year, but didn't have the skills or discipline to go further. I decided I wanted something bigger and better. My goal was to be All-American and to win a National Championship.

I decided I wanted to go to Long Beach State University in beautiful Southern California. They are known for their volleyball program and I wanted to be part of it. Luckily for me, Head Coach Brian Gimmillaro was interested and had a scholarship to offer, so I transferred from ASU to LBSU the summer before my junior year. It was there that I first met Misty May, the other two-time Olympic Gold Medalist in Beach Volleyball and Kerri Walsh's future partner. She was my setter (a volleyball position) in college and she, too, is one of the most incredible and generous people I have ever had the fortune to meet.

The program at Long Beach State was a different experience than I was used to; it was extremely structured. I had trouble finding my way for a while. I kept slipping up and causing problems because everything was monitored; even down to the color of my hair tie at practice. But, I learned and things gradually got better.

Meanwhile, my volleyball skills had reached a new level. I was doing things I didn't even know I was capable of doing and in my junior year, I was invited to the World University Games tryouts at the Olympic Training Center in Colorado Springs. I arrived two weeks late to the training session because I was in summer school. I didn't make the roster because they didn't think it would be fair to replace someone who had participated in the full program with the squad with someone who hadn't.

Back at Long Beach State, our team headed to Japan for pre-season training against their National Champions. I had a falling out with Brian there and almost left the team. There were respect and positive reinforcement issues that I felt needed to be dealt with; thankfully they were resolved.

In my senior year, we went on to a 33-3 record and were ranked #1 in the nation. We made it through the NCAA tournament to the Final Four in Spokane, Washington, where we lost to the eventual champs, Stanford. My friend, Kerri Walsh, was on the other side of the net on the Stanford squad.

I left college in search of a career in professional volleyball. I had dabbled in the beach game with Misty and her dad, Butch, a bit during college, but by the time I graduated college, the AVP Pro Beach Volleyball Tour had gone under; my only option was to play indoor volleyball in Europe.

My first stop was Palermo, Sicily. I was 19 years old and had never been that far from home. I'd grown up in Arizona across town from ASU and LBSU was only a five-hour trip from home. In Sicily, there was no shooting home for the weekend. I missed my family and boyfriend terribly and ended up missing out on an amazing opportunity. I left within the month due to homesickness that was compounded by the language barrier. It was much harder to keep in touch with people back then, too. The internet has become an amazing tool for travelling athletes!

Once home, I realized my huge mistake and regretted my decision to return. So, I contacted my agent again and was sent out the following fall to Istanbul, Turkey. Again, this was a difficult situation since few people there spoke English and it was extremely hard to communicate with anyone. I travelled from team to team, trying out for weeks with my local agent; with no luck. Then, I realized that my agent had his own 'B' level team he wanted me to play for. I wasn't happy with that arrangement due to a decrease in pay. I called my agent in the US and asked him if there was anywhere else and he sent me to Switzerland. I ended up playing in the city of Schauffhausen for the season and enjoyed myself. The pay was enough to live on and I got to play volleyball; which is what I love to do. I thought it wasn't a bad deal, if I do say so myself. But, when I got home I learned that people were making heaps of money playing overseas! I missed out on the cash, but had an incredible experience, so I can't complain.

When I got home, I had no money saved and needed to get a job. There was no money to be earned playing volleyball in Arizona, so I went to work as a bartender; something temporary. I wanted to return to Europe to play, eventually, but had to wait for the next season.

Well, the next season came and went and I continued working; I was making decent money and I was in love. I was getting married. Then life happened and suddenly, three years later, I was divorced and still bartending.

I was working one beautiful Sunday afternoon, zipping through TV channels to find something for my customers to watch when I landed on NBC. To my dismay, there were Misty May and Kerri Walsh, in the finals of an AVP event. I was devastated; all my missed opportunities came rushing back to mock me. I hadn't felt like that since they'd told me I'd have to sit out a year from sports when I'd hurt my knee as a kid. I told everyone in the bar they would just have to wait a few minutes and I went to the office to sulk for a bit. I couldn't believe I'd missed my chance to play the game that I loved so much in order to be sitting in a small bar, serving drinks for the last three years of my life. I had blown it. I was sad and disappointed in myself.

I found out the AVP was coming to Arizona the following season and I went to the event in Tempe. I saw a few friends and said hello to Misty and Kerri; they were just beginning their march on the world at that time.

All through the following year, I kept thinking, "I could have" and, "I should have" but the thought "I will" hadn't entered my mind, yet. The tour came back to town the following year and I met up with Misty and her family for dinner. Suddenly, from out of nowhere, I surprised myself by asking Butch, "What if I wanted to play? What does it take?" He responded by telling me it wasn't worth my time and it was very expensive. AVP athletes have to pay all of their own travel expenses; unlike a pro baseball or football team where it's all covered by the team. Butch also told me that it takes about three years to really understand the game and get good enough to make any money at it.

His noncommittal answers were partially motivated by his memory of me from college; let's just say I enjoyed my college experience to the fullest and made many memories! What he wasn't aware of was my drive and motivation and that I had grown up. All my life I had half-assed things because I could get away with it. But, I had come to a point where I realized that I'd never pushed myself for fear of failure. I'd thought that if I didn't give 100% and failed, I could always tell myself that I could have succeeded if I'd wanted to, since I hadn't really tried. There are many things that I could have excelled at if I had only applied myself. I didn't want to grow old saying, "I bet I could have," about anything in my life.

Jim Steele, a family friend of the May's helped make my dream a reality. He was my liaison with Butch, who wasn't interested in what I was saying because he felt that my fire would pass. With Jim's help, I made plans to meet with Butch and Misty to discuss possible arrangements for coming out and trying to make it at the beach volleyball game.

I drove to California a few weeks after the Arizona event to show that I was serious and got my plan in motion. Everyone was willing to help me get started and find my way. With that meeting under my belt, at the beginning of May, I went home to Arizona, put in my notice to quit my bartending job, sold everything I owned and moved to California five weeks later. Misty opened up her home to me that summer for a few months while she traveled the world, kicking everyone's butt. I eventually found a place and started my new adventure of beach volleyball. My beach volleyball career started out slow and shaky. I played with the Huntington Beach locals everyday to learn how to walk and jump in the sand. They call that getting your 'sand legs.' The entire first summer was spent doing just that. It's amazing how different it is to move in the sand athletically as opposed to a hard surface. Everything is tweaked enough that you almost have to learn each skill over again in a new position. Your center of gravity is different, as well as the angle in which you move. Even learning how to see in the sunlight is straining. I played in three events that summer to learn how the AVP system worked and got a taste of travelling. I finished that season ranked #152. I was on the board!

I spent my first off-season finding a partner and working with trained people. I worked very hard with a group of girls and a coach/trainer for months and I eventually ran into my first partner at one of the local California tournaments not associated with the AVP. Janelle Ruen and I immediately clicked and took the AVP by storm; at least dust devil status.

We started out in Qualifier events that are played the day before each main AVP event. It wasn't until our third event in Santa Barbara that we qualified for the Main Draw event starting the next day. Since we were the lowest ranked team to qualify at that tournament, our first round match was against the #1 ranked team; none other than Misty May and Kerri Walsh! I was excited by the chance to play against my longtime friends. Misty's dad, Butch, joked with me before the match and said, "You want some of this, Jenny?" I replied, "Bring it on, Butch!"

We won the first game! To clarify, a match consists of the best two out of three games. So, needless to say, everyone was a bit shocked that Janelle and I had prevailed in the first game. We went to our player box to get ready for the next game and didn't know what to say. We giggled a bit and I told Janelle then that they were going to be fired up and not to expect the same team to come out. I was right. They handled us pretty easily the next two games to win the match. It was a fun and memorable experience. On a side note: Janelle and I are still the only team in history to win a game against Misty and Kerri in the first round of any tournament.

We improved quickly after that. By midseason, Janelle and I no longer had to qualify; we had earned enough points and finished well enough in previous tournaments to start in the main draw events. That was quite a feat for our first season on the beach. Unfortunately, we made no money and were still paying out of pocket to play. The prize money doesn't trickle down far enough for a player to break even unless they are finishing in the top ten every week.

Janelle and I were happy with our first year and hit the following off-season hard. We got a coach and practiced as often as we could. We started the season with high expectations of continuing what we had started the year before. It turned out to be a letdown! We were reaching so high that we hit the ground pretty hard when we lost our first eight matches in the first four events of the year. To clarify; beach volleyball tournaments use a double elimination format; lose twice and you go home. We didn't know what to do. We tried everything. We finally decided that it would probably be best if we tried to play with different partners for the rest of the season. Though this made us sad, especially since we had become good friends, we knew it was for the best.

Unfortunately, finding someone to partner up with in the middle of the season can be tricky. Not everyone is willing to make a switch. Having that dilemma, Janelle and I played the next event together, knowing we were going to split. Incredibly, we took our first 9th place finish! How exciting! We finally broke through to the top ten; what we'd wanted all along. Because of this, we decided to keep playing together. The next event didn't go as smoothly and we lost two in a row and got knocked out of the tournament. Again, we felt it was best to split. The 9th place finish must have been a fluke and we decided to go our separate ways. The problem remained, however, that there was no one else looking to split at that time. So as to not miss out on any events, we decided to play in one last event together. You guessed it, we took another 9th place. Amazing! But, we stuck to our guns and split. We both jumped around from partner to partner that season, never equaling our best finish of two 9th place finishes. I ended the season ranked #42.

My third year on tour was bumpy. I started out with a great rookie in Whitney Pavlik. We played in five events together and finished 9th three of those five. Our chemistry wasn't the best, however, so we split. I played with a few more people that year and took some more 9th place finishes. I finished off the season with Keao Burdine and had a decent year. I finished last year ranked #32.

I have hit this off-season with so much more knowledge than I had even just a year ago. I'm still learning and will always be a student of the game. It's trial and error; in order to find out what works for my game and keeps my body in the best condition. There are so many factors. I still don't know the right mixture but feel I have the best team I can gather at this point in my life.

I have two wonderful women sponsoring me through their business of Chiropractic/ART and Acupuncture at the Lotus Health Center in Los Alamitos, California. As an athlete, my body gets abused and needs constant maintenance. These women, Dr. Julie Brown and Dr. Camhy Hall, along with weekly yoga and Rett Larson workouts, help keep me in top performance. I started off this season with a talented and experienced player in Diane Pascua. Unfortunately, the trial and error of chemistry is always difficult.

The first few events didn't go as well as we had hoped and I needed to pick up a player with enough points to get into the main draw of a particular event that had no qualifier because Diane didn't have enough points to get us in. I strategically picked up an ambitious and great player by the name of Claire D'Amore for that one event. We ended up playing great and had a great time. She has now become my "Red Hot Pepper Seed" and I believe we will finish out the season together. I am having fun and loving what I do. The paychecks still hurt a little, but the enjoyment of playing outweighs that for now. I will never have this opportunity again. Because of this, the continuing theme is to train hard and give it everything I have. I will never look back on this stage in my life and say, "If only I had..."

I am grateful to have the family, friends and influences in my life that have helped get me to where I am today. Some of those major influences have been my parents, Linda and Mike Templin and Monty and Julie Snyder and my grandma, Anita Snyder. They have supported me in everything I have ever done and will always continue to do so. Without their support no part of my journey would have been possible. To my surprise and delight, in the middle of the quest to be a professional beach volleyball player, I met the love of my life. Lance von Stade has been part of my backbone on this ride for almost three years. Without the help of Lance and my family, this possible 2012 Olympic run wouldn't be the attainable goal that it is for me today. As we like to say, "Onward!!!"

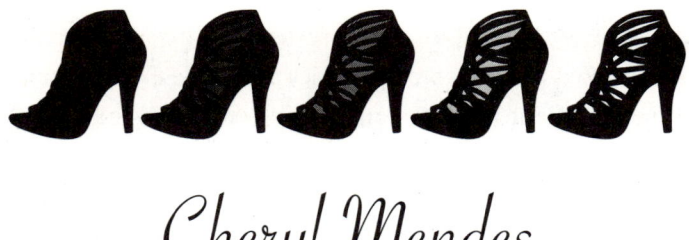

Cheryl Mendes

*I*magine being unhappy with yourself; thinking you could never be beautiful or have a great body. Imagine thinking your life will never get any better and you'll never find the person whom you want to share your life with. Imagine being convinced that even if you did find the person you saw yourself with, they wouldn't be interested in you, because you aren't attractive enough for them.

That used to be me back in grade nine. I thought I could start over with a fresh new look, dress with the best designer labels and hang out with the popular crowd; but I was wrong. I started high school in 1998 and everything I planned on achieving was no more than a dream I thought I could accomplish.

The fresh new look I wanted didn't happen because I didn't have a job, which meant I didn't have the money to purchase the designer labels that I wanted. I hung out with ordinary, everyday people who weren't overly conceited about their looks or fashion or what others thought about them. These were people I knew I could really count on; especially the two I had grown up with and who I still continue to count on, more than 15 years later.

During my first and second years of high school, I tried to set goals for myself that I thought would be easy to achieve, such as joining a sports team, getting better grades and so on. When it came down to achieving the goals I'd set for myself, I realized that it's much easier to set goals and more difficult to achieve them. Before my final years in high school, I really wanted a boyfriend, so I could finally say I had a boyfriend, I wanted a job, my driver's license and a car. By the end of my second year I got my license; passing the test on my first try and in third year, I got a job downtown in telemarketing and a boyfriend. The only goal I never achieved was getting my first car, but that was okay because getting a car was a lot of money and responsibility.

My first boyfriend was an Italian guy in my grade who liked me, but whose existence was unknown to me until a mutual friend or ours pointed him out to me. We started talking and before long we ended up dating. The year we dated was pretty rocky. We broke up and got back together quite frequently. Eventually, I decided that we were just two different people and I ended the relationship permanently at the end of my fourth year of high school.

In my fifth and final year in high school I met a great guy whom I dated during the last year of high school and throughout college. This relationship lasted nearly four years and was the longest relationship I've ever had. I thought that this relationship would eventually lead to marriage but towards the end I realized I wasn't happy and the most important thing to me in a relationship is to be happy so I ended it. This was one of the most difficult things I've ever had to do because I spent four years of my life with him and I was very close to his family.

I feel that experiencing past relationships opens your eyes to what you're really looking for. The experience I got from my past relationships made me realize, I needed to take my time and really look for someone who would make me happy and had the qualities I wanted in someone. I sometimes think back to high school and wonder how different things would have been if I had made different choices or done things differently but then looking at the choices I once made and the things I once experienced is what made me the person I am today.

Starting college was an entirely new experience for me and I graduated with no regrets. I met many wonderful people and what I loved most was that the group I hung around with consisted of people from different races and both genders; that was different for me because in high school, I had only hung around with girls. But in college, I hung out with people who weren't concerned about who they were hanging around with. College was a period of my life where I didn't set goals for myself, but was content to let whatever happened, just happen. I promised myself to have no regrets and to learn from my mistakes and just have fun.

The only blot on my college experience was being diagnosed with epilepsy, a chronic neurological disorder that is characterized by seizures. Epilepsy can usually be controlled, not cured, with medication; although surgery may be considered in severe cases. Epilepsy should not be understood as a single disorder; but rather as a group of syndromes with vastly divergent symptoms, all involving episodic abnormal electrical activity in the brain.

The day I found out that I had epilepsy, I felt as though my world was ruined; that people would look at me differently and no one would want to be with me because of my health problems. Now that I've lived with epilepsy for nearly five years, I've come to realize that there are people out there with far worse health issues then myself; people living with diseases with no cure; young children who are born with disabilities or were in some sort of accident and are now missing a limb. I have come to realize that my seizures can be controlled with pills; I would now have to take these pills for the rest of my life, but the seizures could be controlled. Those realizations brought home to me the fact that epilepsy couldn't stop me from pursuing my goals and having everything I wanted. It was just something I learned to deal with and in the end, I won.

After coming to terms with my health, I finished college and joined a dance class where I learned how to salsa dance. Four years later, I am still continuing to learn and plan on doing so for a lot longer. Before graduating, I ended up getting a job in a freight forwarding company where I lasted for nearly three years and then later decided to put my education to good use and pursue a career in marketing. I got a job I loved at a great company, Deloitte and Touche, and was extremely happy I got in because many people want to work for this company. They have a lot of advantages to offer to their employees.

In the summer of 2008, I joined a co-ed baseball team and signed up for hip hop lessons. These were things I've always wanted to do, but never pushed myself previously. After adjusting to epilepsy, everything else I wanted to do was easy to accomplish.

If I now look back at my life, I realize I've accomplished a lot. I've done many things I've always wanted to do and learned from my many mistakes. I am proud of the woman I now am. I now sponsor two kids from India; one boy and a girl, I volunteer and organize many charity events, try to help others when I can and don't hold myself back when I want to accomplish something.

If I've learned anything, it's that you only live once and you should make the most of it. Never let anyone stand in the way of your going after what you want. When you feel down, always remember that people are in worse situations then yourself and be grateful for the blessings that you have. Have faith in yourself and believe that you are strong enough to pick yourself up when you're down and not only continue but learn from your mistakes. Life is short; make the most of what you have and live everyday as if it were your last.

Daniela Godoy Jameson Cruz

Sometimes the best gift in life is to give to others and to put your own needs second; when you can do this, you can be truly happy. Why? Sometimes, forgetting about yourself can be the key to happiness; when you're too self absorbed, you can have too much time to critique yourself and self destruct. To avoid such behaviour, I began volunteering when I was sixteen. I would pick certain projects and put my heart and soul into them; it was very rewarding. I started to feel very self assured and I was content.

However, after I graduated from high school, I had no sense of direction. I applied to three universities and got accepted to all of them; making it even more difficult for me to decide what it was that I wanted. I knew I wanted something big; I couldn't believe some people had such lame goals as buying houses and starting families. To me, that was boring; just a small part of life and not the big picture. I entered the philosophy and communications project at York University. At the same time, I decided that I wanted to become a real estate agent, however while concentrating on my university studies; I failed the real estate exam.

During university, I was *Miss Hispanidad* second runner up; *Miss Diverse Canada* first runner up; *Miss Latina Canada* Queen 2005 and I made the top ten in *Miss Latina World*. My first pageant had been in my homeland Argentina in 2000, where I had won *Miss Liceo Militar Espejo*. Pageants made me very competitive and I believed competition bred quality because it forced me to develop my best abilities and qualities.

However, in spite of all my success, I felt like a loser because I had failed my phase one real estate exam. No matter how many achievements I garnered from school and my social life; that failed real estate exam haunted me. I never tried writing it again. I began working for a call centre that encouraged me to become a licensed life insurance agent, but once again, I failed the exam. Friends encouraged me to try both the real estate exam and the life insurance exam again, but I soon realized that I just wasn't interested in the subject matter. I had forced myself to try to achieve things because others had recommended them, but I hadn't considered what I wanted. I sometimes wondered what I was doing and why was I just doing things and not focusing on university. I felt like I wanted to achieve as much as I could in the shortest time possible. I was sitting on many chairs at the same time. Worst of all, I was confused.

For a woman to be confused in our century is no surprise. We are told that we can be whatever we want to be; whether that is a doctor, engineer, astronaut or mechanic. Our ancestors were limited to careers as teachers, secretaries or nurses; now we have more choices and more opportunities. There are virtually no limits to what a woman can do; therefore our confusion can be great.

I was confused; I changed my major to philosophy and translation and kicked communications. I was fluent in three languages and believed translation would be a great choice. Failing the life insurance exam made me feel like a loser and brought back memories of the real estate exam. I didn't want to tell anyone; I was so ashamed. People congratulated me and told me they were proud of my university education and of all the pageants, events and film work I was doing on the side while working a part time job. But, all I thought about were those lousy exams I hadn't passed. I just hated the feeling of failure. With pageants it was different, I had won my first pageant and once you've had a taste of that winning feeling, you don't really taste the losing feeling.

While I was *Miss Latina Canada*, I decided to help others again. I was meeting a lot of people, doing a lot of networking and garnering a lot of attention and I wanted to use the opportunity for something good. I started *Toyz Love International* from the bedroom of my home. I gathered all the teddy bears and toys I could get my hands on and sent them back home to Argentina for the poor kids who had nothing for Christmas. I wanted to continue on a bigger scale, so I staged an event with my local church and raised enough toys to fill a 40-foot container; I paid the shipping from my own pocket and sent it.

I was very frustrated and disappointed to learn that the container was stopped at customs and never delivered to the orphanage to which it was intended. Even putting some lawyers on the case was ineffectual. I had put a great deal of time and effort into the project and I was extremely disillusioned with the result.

There followed a dark period of my life. I had managed to find a full time job before I finished university. This was a double-edged sword; one the one hand, I was more financially secure but, it then became necessary for me to finish my schooling on a part time basis and it took twice as long. I fell into a rut. A car accident, a broken heart, being rejected from many auditions and the death of my nephew pushed my rut into a full blown depression. I managed to graduate while working a full time job and doing film, hosting events, filming commercials, TV shows and modeling. I felt that what I had studied wasn't practical so I enrolled at Humber College for their Project Management Course and graduated.

I felt I had gained new skills. I struggled hard and when I finished, I had a university degree, a college diploma, a great network of people and I felt miserable. I tried looking at all the different careers available and nothing appealed to me. I felt lazy and like I wasn't living; I was merely existing. When I went to sleep I was happy because I wanted to dream; reality wasn't as exciting. Rejection phase kicked into my life where no matter where I applied it was, "No sorry, the position has been filled," or, "we've decided to go in another direction."

I felt that rejection was my second name; that whether it be for an audition or for a job, nobody wanted me. I felt miserable, unlucky and like a reject; I was mad at the world and myself. Competition was fierce out there, no matter what you wanted to do and I felt as if I wasn't good enough. I wanted to hide from the world and stay in my own bubble. The stress and anxiety started to affect me on a physical level.

I left my job. With my small savings and a few gigs and lots of prayers and hope, I started recovering from an exhausting phase. I started to ask myself who I was, what I wanted and what made me happy. I started going through my past and I found lots of things, to my surprise, which had made me happy as a child. I had enjoyed the creative arts; acting, photography, and writing. I decided to pursue these interests with my entire soul. I love helping others because I can forget about my own problems.

I started working more vigorously on the charity I had started in 2005; *Toyz Love International.* This humanitarian work was a passion for me and I smiled when I did it. My previous experience and knowledge helps me run my charity; so it wasn't all in vain after all. Finally, I organized a fundraiser which became a success and which I now look forward to every year. We don't send 40-foot containers full of toys anymore; I learned an expensive and painful lesson there. We send money now. Every single penny we make we send and there are no customs agents waiting on the other end to take the money. This has been my biggest achievement, so far. I don't want to be big anymore myself, but I want to make my charity big, because its positive effect would be big where it is most needed. I put my heart and soul through an emotional rollercoaster and I had many stops which affected me, changed me and shaped me; nevertheless I stood up and my life has been a salad of rejections, but it doesn't matter anymore because when I am rejected, someone else is winning and someone else deserves a chance.

Shelby Way

*H*ave you ever got up in the morning and thought, "I hate my job and I don't want to go to work." Or have you ever wondered, "What am I doing with my life?" Well I have! I liked some of the jobs and places I've worked, but I always knew they were for the time being; to pay the bills. I've done all kinds of different jobs; donut shop employee, security guard at a mall and at a hotel, cashier at a grocery store and gas station, receptionist, cook, waitress, bartender, pool attendant, golf course attendant and personal trainer.

When I was 16, I lived with my father who was very ill with cancer. It was just the two of us and I took care of him. Unfortunately, he lost his battle in March of 1998 and I went to live with my grandparents. I had a good job at the time that I worked at after school and on weekends. They needed someone fulltime, so I ended up leaving school; I wasn't going anywhere with my education after losing my father anyway. I was working a lot, so I decided to move out of my grandparents and into my own place. I was 17.

Although I was living on my own and had a good job, I still wasn't sure what I wanted to do for the rest of my life. I thought about going back to school, but needed to keep working. I would change jobs when better ones came along, but never found the right one.

That started to change a little over five years ago. I was living with my fiancé and his two children; being a stay-at-home stepmom. It was okay, but I still felt like I was missing something. I loved those children, but I needed something for me, too. I've always wanted my own business, but what?

One day, while I was doing a friend's hair and we were talking about my problem, she suggested that I should be a hairstylist. I had never thought of doing that! I'd often done hair for some of my friends and family members, but that was just to help them out. Suddenly, though, it seemed like a good idea. So I started looking into some schools and it seemed more and more like something I'd really like to do. I enrolled at *Bruno's School of Hair Design* in September of 2004. The course was ten months long and when I finished, I worked with a friend who had been doing hair for years. I also continued to do family and friends hair and began to develop a client base. Now I knew the business I wanted to have!

In April of 2006, I started to look around for space to lease. A family member introduced me to someone who had some space, so I met with him to check it out. After looking around, I didn't find anything else that I liked better. The space was a large 1800 square feet; it was in a great location and it was completely gutted so I could start from scratch and do whatever I wanted with it. Plus, the owner offered me a great deal and promised to help with some of the renovations. I gave him a deposit and he worked on the lease while I started looking for a contractor. I couldn't believe it! Things seemed to be falling into place and my dream of owning my own business was starting to look like a reality!

I was enjoying my holidays in August of that year when I got some devastating news. The building that housed my future salon had been in a fire. There was a restaurant attached to my space and that's where it had started. I was crushed; my dreams had literally gone up in flames. The only good news was that I hadn't started construction yet.

I didn't know what to do; whether I should start looking for a new space or wait until the building was cleared by the fire marshals and insurance company. Who knew how long that would take? No one would be allowed to do work on the building until they were done and gave the all clear. I began looking around for a new property, just in case, but again I didn't find anything I liked; I had my heart set on the first building. I decided to wait. Well the summer ended; then the fall, Christmas and New Years was over and still I had no idea when I'd be able to get going on my salon.

In the meantime, I was going through some tough times at home. My fiancé and I were having problems. I decided to make a huge life change and move out and to another city. It was one of the hardest things I've ever had to do. I'd been with this person for almost 6 years and his children were like my own. Shortly after moving out in May of 2007, I got more devastating news. The owner of the building that I hoped would house my salon informed me that because he hadn't been allowed to make any repairs to the roof of the building, rain and snow had caused black mold. You can't just remove black mold; the building would have to be torn down. I couldn't believe what I was hearing; again, I was crushed.

So now what? I had left my family and moved to another city. Now I didn't have space for my business or a job. I considered just getting another job for the time being or working at another salon and forgetting about my own. But, I didn't want to go work at another job that I knew I would hate and I didn't want to go to another salon.

I decided to take the summer off, work as the pool attendant at the building where I live, do hair out of my apartment, mend my broken heart and figure out what to do.

It turned out to be the best thing I could have done. I decided to keep trying for my own salon. I continued to work out of my home and at my clients' homes while looking for a new space. I wasn't going to give up. I'd been through too much to just give in. I began looking around again, but this time I was going to take my time and find the perfect spot.

One day, while I was on my way to the bank down the street from where I lived, I noticed a 'for lease' sign in one of the stores in the nearby plaza. A few days later, I met with the realtor and took a look at two available spaces. The first one was too small, but the second was perfect. It was the same size as my original space; 1800 sq ft. When I walked through the door, I could see exactly how my salon would look; something just felt right about the space. I called the realtor a week later and told him that I wanted it and to start working on the lease.

The next step was getting to the bank for a loan. I had some money saved, but nothing near what I was going to need. I applied for a small business loan. There was a lot that needed to be done for that. I had to complete a business plan; thankfully, I have a friend that works in a bank and was able to help me with it. I also needed an estimate from a contractor and I needed to price out all the supplies and furniture, etc. When I suddenly learned that the bank wasn't going to be lending me as much as they had originally promised, it became necessary for me to go to family for a co-signer. I had really wanted to do it all on my own, but sometimes we all need a helping hand.

In May of 2008, construction finally began! I couldn't believe it was actually happening. So many times I had thought my dream was dead and was never going to come true. It was amazing to see this big empty space being turned into my salon, step by step. Then, it was time to hire staff and start advertising the opening. I put ads in the local papers and beauty supply stores. I got lots of resumes and started arranging interviews. I knew right away the people that I wanted and the ones I didn't. I had thought it would be hard because I'd never hired staff before, but it turned out to be easy; I just followed my gut.

The construction was moving along quickly. Soon, it was time to start getting supplies and furnishing the space. That part was easy because I knew exactly what I wanted. The furniture was being custom built and would be delivered when everything else was finished. I spent a lot of time putting together shelves and other spaces for storage.

I was so consumed with all the things that needed to be done and the decisions that I had to make that it wasn't until the construction was done and the furniture and supplies were set up that I realized that it was really happening and I was getting close to opening! All the work was done, I'd hired all my staff and the only thing left to do was decide the best day to open. I had a staff meeting to find out what would be best for everyone and to make sure that all the final details were attended to and that everyone had everything they needed. We decided on August 12/2008.

As it got closer to the opening, I got more excited and nervous. I started having doubts and second-guessing myself. What would I do if no one came? I had put everything I had into my new venture. I had provided jobs for other people, including family. It was a lot of pressure, but at the same time, it was something I believed in. I also believed in myself and sometimes you just have to go for it. It'll never happen if you don't try. I also had the love and support of my family and friends.

When the day of the grand opening arrived, I was so excited to finally rip the paper off the windows, put the open sign up and reveal my beautiful salon. It was August, so a lot of people were still on holidays and it was pretty slow. But everyone knew that would happen; it was good to be open, anyway. We got a rhythm going for when it would be busy. It also gave us all time to get to know each other. Again, I put ads in the paper, got a huge lawn sign and advertised in local beauty supply stores.

It's been almost a year now and things have changed dramatically. We are much busier now. My staff is amazing and we're all very close; we're more like family than staff. It's hard when times are slow because the bills don't stop coming, but I keep reminding myself that we're still new and it takes time to get your name out there. As the old saying goes, "Rome wasn't built in a day!" People will always need their hair done and I have a fantastic, very talented staff. People always come back! Word of mouth is the best kind of advertising!

Sometimes when I walk into the salon, I still can't believe that it's mine and that my dream has come true. I finally feel like I'm doing what I was meant to do and that's a great feeling. It's taken a lot for me to get where I am and many times I've doubted that it would ever happen and wanted to give up. I really believe that what doesn't kill you will make you stronger and sometimes when one door slams in your face, another one opens. At one point, I really thought that I wasn't meant to open a salon and have my own business. I see now that I wasn't meant to open a salon in the first space and while I was in the relationship I was in. I was meant to do it on my own.

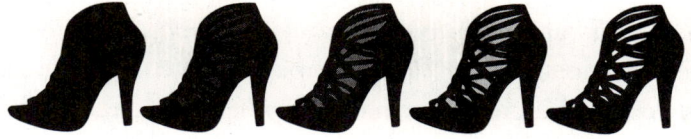

Ariel Garten

Say yes to yourself. It's not an easy thing to do. Our brains are actually constantly inhibiting. It's a strange thing to wrap your mind around. Our movement system, for example, is in a constant state of inhibition. Often, it's only when you inhibit the inhibition that your body can perform a willful movement; odd as that may seem. That's why in many movement disorders people end up with tremors- uncontrollable movements- a breakdown in the standard, constant, self inhibition that our brains are under.

When one sustains damage to the prefrontal cortex- the thinking and planning parts- the most commonly observed abnormal behaviours are problems with inhibition: blurting out, running through the streets naked, vulgar behaviour. We are taught to be very composed and reserved; very inhibited. It's part of our fundamental wiring.

That's great if you're in Victorian England or wish to impress your new in-laws with your polite behaviour. It's not so great when our own self-inhibition, or inner critic, stands in the way of getting what we want. "I can't do it," or "that's beyond me," or "I don't deserve this, it's for someone else; not me," are the best ways to think if you don't want to live out your dreams.

I went through a great struggle trying to write this book chapter. Okay, so it wasn't my greatest struggle; but it was significantly harder than I thought it was going to be. So much so that I almost didn't write it and missed the deadline. I had a very nasty little goon get in my way; the inner critic. In this case, he was disguised in a sneaky form; the perfectionist. I'd set out night after night to write my chapter, only get a few words down and then stare off into space. I'd cancel dinner plans so I could write and end up doing a bang-up job of returning emails for rentals clients until, "oh, look, it's bedtime, better do that because I wouldn't want to screw up tomorrow, when I might actually write..." Why was I procrastinating so? It didn't have to be perfect; as a therapist, I know that nothing is ever perfect and the scourge of aiming for perfection can lead to a life of dissatisfaction. But I wanted it to be damn good. That desire kept me from actually being able to create anything.

Does that sound familiar? "But perfectionism is a *good* thing," you might say. Wanting to make things good is important, I agree; but the pressure to excel can be stultifying. You have to know that the ability to do good work is in you; it flows naturally. When you don't have an inner critic telling you it won't be good enough, then what you sit down and do *will* be good enough; it will be a natural and honest expression of you.

Most of us keep that sinister inner critic around because we believe him to be useful. We think that if he tells us we are doing badly, it will motivate us to do better; but it doesn't. Hearing that voice only saps us of motivation. The inner critic doesn't motivate you; no matter how much he has convinced you that he does. He only makes it harder to work freely and clearly at the task at hand. Think about one thing that your inner critic said to you today. It might be something like, "you're stupid," or "my hair's a mess." Now imagine someone saying the same thing to you or your best friend. How would you react? You'd want to defend your friend and you'd be mortified and insulted; even more so if the comments were directed to you. Yet, we accept these things all day long from the voice in our heads; we've gotten so used to that voice, we don't even question it.

Why is it okay to abuse ourselves with this language? The truth is; it's not. But, we often don't know any better and assume because this is the way it is, it's the way it should be.

So what can you do to get this voice to stop bugging you? Imagine what it would be like to be free of that draining, detracting, pernicious voice in your head... Quite liberating, I'm sure. Give a shape and a name to your inner critic; pull him out of your head and put him on the wall.

Now, that your inner critic is out in the open and seen for what he is, let him have it. This guy has been getting in your way and screwing up your day for too long. He has no right to do that! Tell him that. Shrink him on the wall; make him small before you tell him that again. Tell him to get lost; that you do *not* need him. You might have thought he was helping you until now or just felt guilty so you kept him around, but now you can see he's a useless drain of energy and you will *take no more of it!*

Other than when this voice pops into my head, I've had a life that is otherwise free of struggle, for the most part. This freedom is truly characterized by the lack of the inner critic.

In high school, I had a very creative flair and the word on the street was that I wore a different outfit to school every day for four years. From polyester 70's *Ginger* from *Gilligan's Island* gowns, to swirling 60's psychedelic minidresses with matching stockings and platforms, to fishnet creations comprised mainly of four pairs of hose and some scissors. I was quite out there and somehow luckily managed to be on the fringe and be respected. I had friends from many different social cliques beside my core friend group and I was respected, rather than ostracized, for my daring.

A lack of social anxiety definitely helped my social standing; having good, confident thoughts about myself and the social outcomes allowed me to act gregarious and socially comfortable.

My fun with fashion led me to realize one day that I had made a T-shirt that was easily reproducible and possibly popular, so I made several of them and set off to Queen Street to sell them. I took my little line of T-shirts in a shopping bag from store to store and heard no after no, but I remained unfazed. After about a dozen rejections, someone took them on consignment. Whoa, suddenly I was a clothing designer! Had I attended to the thoughts of a defeating voice at any point along the way, who knows if I could have ever made it past the second store to reject me. A few months later, I did the same thing with a second simple shirt and after another round of rejections, I actually sold half a dozen.

A few summers later, I was in New York on a summer stint as a very junior designer for Club Monaco. I did the same thing with the stores in New York; receiving forty 'no thank you's' instead of the usual ten, before making a sale. Now I was a designer selling in New York City.

At the same time, on the school front, I pursued the sciences; loving them. I eventually pioneered a biotechnology program in our school. I was also busy acting in the school productions, as well as designing sets and costumes for the plays and student designing the big annual fashion show. I was able to successfully accomplish so much by never thinking that I couldn't. If you try, generally you can. And not giving in to any conventional idea of limitations. In my final year of high school, I got a position in a research lab.

To me, art and science were not parts of a world divided; that was a conventional barrier, a story that we tell ourselves. Creativity and follow-through are a key element to both. In university, I majored in sciences, deciding that I could and would be trained in clothing design later. Eventually, I fell in love with neuroscience; which explains not just how things work, but how *we* work. I also continued to pursue my clothing label while in university. I expanded my line and ran an art gallery out of my living room while I grew Parkinson's disease model neurons in Petri dishes. When I graduated, I figured it was time to take clothing design seriously, since I had just spent the last four years in science.

Rather than go back to school for another four years of design training, I smashed through the wall of a bedroom in my ground floor apartment on trendy College St. I sketched out a full line and took it to a dressmaker I found through an ad in the paper and all of a sudden, I was a bona fide designer with my own retail store.

The store, *Flavour Hall*, was a huge hit. I promoted other design labels, expanded my own line and distribution to 30 stores across North America. I acquired sales agents and a team of seamstresses and we exhibited in *Toronto Fashion Week* every season with shows that "revolutionized the runway." In only my third year of business, we opened *Fashion Week* and were featured in over a dozen print and television spots.

I accomplished all of that without a single business course, any formal design training or the ability to sew a skirt well. It didn't matter.

In retrospect, what did matter was my determination and the knowledge that I could succeed. So I did it; and so can you. Just try and try consistently and if that voice gets in your way, tell it to F-off; it has no right.

After four years of clothing design, I realized that I wanted to continue with neuroscience and that fashion couldn't easily scale up to accommodate the standard of living I envisioned for myself and an eventual family. I closed my store and waited for the next thing to hit… and waited. I knew I'd work it out; whatever I did was successful. But still I waited …

So, I took a massage course, thinking that if I was ever broke and forty, with two kids, I could do treatments in my basement to make a living. At the massage course, I met a woman who had taken a course in Neuro-linguistic programming and I did a session with her. It was amazing; I took the NLP course myself. A lot of subsequent training in different methodologies combined with my psychology and neuroscience degree enabled me to become a psychotherapist.

Three years later, I have a completely successful therapy practice, where I have the honour of walking hand-in-hand with people through the parts of themselves that they're afraid of; clearing away the barriers so that they can live the successful lives they wish for.

Meanwhile, I had begun working with a guy who was the inventor of the wearable computer and we had executed a variety of art exhibits together; including one that gave me the excuse to have a Jacuzzi on the lawn in front of my store for a week. Another exhibit saw 48 participants in the audience hooked up to EEG machines so that they could control the outcome of a musician's output from synthesized instruments. In other words, a brainwave controlled concert.

I returned to the brainwave control system later and decided to take it seriously. Last year, I formed a technical and business team and my own thought controlled computing company; aiming to create installations and consumer products. We were very quickly having meetings with the biggest agencies in the world and found ourselves featured in a front-page article in the *Toronto Star;* which led us to stories on several national TV networks. That, in turn, led to the Ministry of Research and

Innovation inviting us to be the showcase of their innovations awards.

When we sat down to create installations with the system, we began to envision our dream presentation venue and we came up with the Olympics. We suggested the idea of a giant thought controlled sculpture to someone at the Space network, who got excited so we put together a proposal. We heard nothing back. After much foot-dragging, I diffidently sent the proposal to a woman who had called me for real estate advice and who had something to do with the Olympics. Again, I heard nothing. I asked the representative from the Ministry of Research and Innovation about the Olympics. She said, "We can look into that."

It took me about one more day to realize that my inner critic voice was getting in my way. I shut him down and emailed off the proposal to the Ministry. Two days later, we heard back that they were very excited about the proposal. They had a list of questions that began with, "Can you do it in Ontario's colours?"

Yes, we can definitely do it in blue. This week, I found out that we were enthusiastically approved for a big installation at the 2010 Olympics in the pavilion; with a potential budget of a quarter million dollars. It pays to follow your dreams and free yourself from the struggle that only you create. Tonight, I sat down and wrote this chapter in one passionate sitting. Be yourself and be okay with yourself.

Bianca Gross

The plane was taking me far away; to the Far East, to be exact. I'd like to say that I didn't even know what had led me to be on that plane; but I did. I had made a mistake and tried to be consistent. But, I wasn't too worried because I knew that this trip would bring me back to myself. I was a person who believed that the only consistency in life is inconsistency.

When I was a young girl, I always wanted to be someone important. I wasn't sure what I would do that would gain me that status, but I was sure that it was going to be something big. I dreamed of becoming a doctor, a lawyer or even an acrobat. I went through phases of wanting to be a hairstylist, a club owner, and a veterinarian. You name it; at some point, I have wanted to be it.

When I graduated from The University of Western Ontario with a BA in International Studies, I went straight into customer service for my family's company; putting aside anything I had learned about the world through my classes. I eventually became bored and decided to 'gopher' at a television station. I was also modeling on the side and one day, I was scouted to work for a promotional company.

That job was great. It had me bouncing around, sampling new products to people all over the city. But eventually, this too became consistent and I decided to take time off and travel. I went to Australia, Thailand, Hong Kong and Japan. It was an experience that will stay with me forever. Upon my return, I wanted to change my life. I felt I was older and wiser and I was sure that it was time to get serious and settle down. I stayed in promotions, but decided to expand into event planning; something that came very naturally to me and I thought I could do it for a long time without getting bored.

Shortly after starting this attempt at consistency, I met Glen. I had actually known him from my university days, but now something was different. He had been working for a couple of years, had grown up, gotten a hair cut and he had become extremely appealing to me.

We had a great time together. I had never known anyone like him; so kind, but with a wild side. Most people felt that Glen and I were two of a kind; I actually thought we were complete opposites. He would probably have said that we were similar; but our differences were the good kind because they complement one another. That's Glen; the eternal optimist who sees the good in everyone. As much as I love him for this positive thinking; it also drove me bananas.

I am a realist. I grew up in a home where the truth was never held back to spare someone's feelings. If dad didn't look good with his new haircut, mom's dinner was overcooked or my toes weren't perfectly pointed during my gymnastic routine, it was said! There was no pussy-footing around. I believe this is referred to as brutal honesty.

My father, a brilliant businessman, is the most generous, kind and loving man in the world. But he has opinions that are unstoppable. Mom wakes up everyday with a smile on her face, ready to make all the people around her happy. Her love for her family shines as bright as the sun but, she too, has strong views on life.

I'm not going to blame my inconsistencies on my opinionated parents, but I will say that's its hard to figure out what you want when you're being told that your aspirations don't fit in with the family's vacation schedule. Don't get me wrong; I love my blunt and honest parents and I continue to love this honesty as an adult; so much so that I too, have become the brutally honest type. If the truth hurts, too bad; it's the truth! Life is too short to hold your breath and bite your tongue. If you care about someone, you say what's on your mind; even if it's going to hurt their feelings, you say it anyway. If you try your hardest and fail, so what; do it again. Or do something else. There's no sulking or pouting allowed. Keep your head up, move on. "It is what it is!" As Dad likes to say. This statement has remained with me over the years and it may only be a few short words strung together, I have an unbelievable attachment to its meaning.

It's probably that attitude of, "it is what it is" that has caused me to bounce around so much. I've never been able to commit to anything for an extended period of time. Whether it is school, work, relationships or travel, I always seem to get bored. The only thing I've ever really committed to is taking care of my Chihuahuas, Martini and Kobe. Those two little dogs make me smile everyday; no matter what is going on. They are my consistency. Everything else is what it is. If I don't like something, I stop doing it. If I don't like where I am, I leave. For some reason, I've never had a problem with this coming and going.

The only person who ever told me that I needed to work on my inconsistencies was Glen. It wasn't a huge problem, but he would bring it up once in a while. He would say that, rather than work on things, I just move on. The funny thing is, I don't disagree; I just don't think it's a big deal. I think it is what it is.

After a short courtship, Glen and I became heavily involved for three years. We traveled, we laughed and we partied like rock stars! Our relationship was what dreams were made of. We never fought, we spent all our free time with one another and we just loved life together!

But as I said, I thought we were complete opposites and that was something that irked me from the beginning of our relationship. I secretly worried that settling down would be hard for me; but I loved him so much, I pushed those doubts aside. After three years, Glen became very busy at work. Life shifted and our priorities changed. I've always liked to move around a lot, so I decided to leave Glen alone for a time and visit with my family in the US. That was a defining moment, according to him. In his eyes, the going was getting tough and I was going to get going. At the time, I didn't see it that way. He never asked me to stay and I assumed it was okay to go. In hindsight, I'll admit that that was the first mistake of many. But that was the one he will never forgive me for.

Throughout our relationship, we had had our victories and struggles; but we had always loved one another. After almost four years together, we decided to get married. We planned a beautiful wedding with all the showstoppers. We worked hard on a new condo that we would call our first home. We booked an elaborate honeymoon and began to plan the rest of our lives together. It all sounded good, but my inner voice was screaming out that I wasn't ready to make that kind of commitment. My husband was perfect, though. Something had to be wrong with me if I was freaking out. People said it was cold feet; that the first year of marriage is very difficult. But I knew I loved Glen. I knew that I had the perfect man who was virtually flawless. So what the $*&@ was wrong?

After much soul searching, I finally realized that none of my doubts were about the relationship or even about my husband; they were all about me and my insecurities, my fear of consistency and predictability. So, I had a meltdown. I made mistakes #5, 6, 7, 8 and 9. I forgot to be true to myself and honest to my husband. I lost track of all the mistakes I made; there were so many. I focused on trying to fix things; when I should have been fixing me. As a result, my marriage became estranged not long after its inception.

Many aspects of my life haven't worked out and I've been mostly okay with that. But this was different because I thought I really wanted to be married. It was time for me to take a long, hard look in the mirror. I had really had it all. So what was missing from my life that was making me so unhappy in a situation that most people would be thriving in?

I have spent the better part of 2009 searching for my truth; soul searching, if you will. I have been in therapy, I have vacationed with friends and I have spent time alone. I've had moments of utter clarity; followed by absolute depression. I was once the girl who was up for anything; but that became a distant memory. I became the girl who couldn't get her key in the door fast enough so as to not break down in tears in her hallway. The girl who couldn't enjoy time with the people she loves. I stopped planning events for fear that I couldn't create a good party anymore. I stopped going out so that people couldn't ask me questions. I basically retreated from my normal world, feeling embarrassed that my marriage had fallen apart. I had lost my outgoing self because I had lost my confidence.

One morning, while lying awake in bed, my thoughts brought me back to university. Usually when I thought of my school days, I thought of the parties, the sorority and the social scene that had encompassed my life at that time. But that morning, it was my studies that were on my brain. I thought back to when I was learning about third world countries and their struggles. About culture and religion, and about all the places around the globe whose problems made my big country of Canada's seem like a utopian paradise. I immediately got up and knew what I had to do.

I decided to search online for volunteer opportunities in the third world. I came across Habitat for Humanity's Global Village Program and applied to go to Cambodia to build homes. The rest happened very quickly. I received a phone call, had an interview, packed my bags and I was off. I didn't need to think about it; it just felt right.

The moment I sat in my seat on the plane, it hit me that what I was doing and where I was headed, was going to change me. I became scared, anxious and overwhelmed. I was hopeful and optimistic about my travels; but I was uncertain that I would find what I was looking for. I called my parents before take off and cried to them about my fears. They reminded me that this experience, if nothing else, could only enrich my soul and allow me to see another side of life. They told me that if I came home still confused, that would be okay. They were so proud of my decision to help the less fortunate and they supported me, no matter what I would or wouldn't find for myself. That was exactly what I needed to hear and with that, my tears stopped and I braced myself for the 20-hour journey.

Upon arrival in Cambodia's capital, Phnom Penh, I instantly realized how far away from home I was. The streets were littered with people, bicycles, mopeds and trash. Children without clothing were everywhere, running, playing and even working. The streets were filthy and cluttered with vendors selling everything from fruit and insects, to clothing. But despite this, I noticed one thing almost immediately; although destitute, the Cambodian people seemed happy. They didn't seem to feel unfortunate at all. Their attitude was so inspiring that our egos and vanity were quickly put aside. The team had a purpose and that was to help these lovely people.

Onsite, the conditions were harsh. There were dirty water ponds everywhere, but the houses were on dry land. The people were really nice and helpful, but very, very poor. The children were always laughing, playing and running all around the work site. They were unbelievably cute and very interested in us. There were also dogs everywhere. They were very unclean and some looked quite ill. In spite of all of that, the overall atmosphere on the site was very positive and hopeful. Habitat had already built many houses in this particular village and the locals had gotten used to having foreigners around. That is not to say that we could do what we wanted. We still had to respect the Cambodian culture by not shaking hands, playing loud music or showing too much skin, among other things.

Building a home was definitely something that I wasn't used to. Aside from the fact that I had never done any construction; in Cambodia, I was doing it without real tools or machinery. Anything was possible though and everything that we did use or create was simple, yet efficient and effective. After ten days, we were dirty, heat stricken and exhausted. But, seeing the faces of the local people when the house was complete was worth every bead of sweat that we put into it.

The last day on the site was very emotional for me. Habitat had a dedication ceremony, where we presented the homeowners with their new home. Two monks and a priest also came to bless the house with a thirty minute Buddhist ceremony. Although I am not a religious person and I couldn't understand any of the prayers, I knew we were all feeling the same thing; thankful.

After the ceremony, the homeowner gave a speech on behalf of himself and his family. It was translated as such, "You all did something good. So many people give money and make donations, but you are the ones who came and did the work. You didn't care to get dirty and sweat in the heat. You came and met us and spent time with us. You didn't just give your money, but you gave your time and your lives. For this, you can never be forgotten." I had never really thought of it that way, but he was right. We did something very selfless in a world full of ego. The funny thing is; it felt perfectly natural.

My experience in Cambodia was nothing short of fantastic, but throughout the trip, in moments of solitude, I couldn't help but remember my struggles back home. I had my moments of sadness, where I remembered that my marriage had fallen apart and that I was separated. I worked hard to keep my head up and I reminded myself that all things happen for a reason. I looked to my fellow team members for support and to the people of Cambodia for inspiration. I focused on the family that I was helping and the beautiful children always laughing and playing in the village. Slowly, but surely, my confidence returned.

My Habitat trip was more than an experience for me; it was an adventure. It brought me back to where I needed to be; back to myself. It reminded me that love and beauty are all around, all the time. That sometimes a plan is not always the answer. We may not know what our tomorrow will bring and that's okay because it is these inconsistencies in life that make us stronger. But most importantly, it showed me that everybody has a story of struggle, but with one another, we can do anything.

As for my future, it's hard to tell. I do know that I will continue to live in the moment and do the things that make me happy. Hopefully, I can inspire others and bring happiness into their lives, too. We all have our problems, but at the end of the day, it is what it is. Only we have the ability to turn it around.

Dr. Biljana Durickovic BSc, DC

*L*ying flat on my back, staring at the low-hanging ceiling of the dingy basement I called home, I was paralyzed with pain due to a damaged disc in my lower back, with a career that wasn't going anywhere. The irony of being a chiropractor with a bad back wasn't lost on me. Nor was the fact that I had more education than 95% of the population, but was making an average of $2.50 an hour; and that was on a good day. This wasn't the way it was supposed to be. I thought back to how it all started.

Graduation day had held so much promise; after eight years of university, I could finally call myself doctor and start my career. Sure, I had student debt the size of a mortgage and would have to build my chiropractic practice one patient at a time, but I was young, invincible and determined.

Less than a year later, my debt had grown, my business was in ruins and my body had betrayed me. I had no prospects, no money and no hope.

After graduating, I felt the urgency to begin working because of the debt load that was weighing heavily on me. Like many of the other students in my class, I'd only been given a grace period of six months between graduation and my first loan payment. I knew that my mother would always be there to support me, but she had done so for many years and I was reluctant to become a financial burden on her or the man who would become my husband, Mark. As a result, I chose two opportunities that just weren't right for me.

I worked long hours and had little to show for it. In an eight hour day, I might only see one or two patients, but I had to remain at the office; what if someone called or walked in and I wasn't there? The patients I had weren't even covering the rent and I was going further into debt everyday.

On top of my mounting financial fears, I was faced with the sad reality that my body wasn't invincible. Many chiropractic techniques involve using one's own body as a counterweight to the patient's. It's very hard on the body of the practitioner; in spite of my light patient load, it wasn't long before my back started to ache. My response was to keep working. What choice did I have? A sore back wasn't going to pay the rent or put food on the table. So, I sucked it up and kept on heading to the office.

The pain continued, however and on a couple of occasions, I hurt my back quite severely. I was fortunate that it always seemed to happen right before a weekend; giving me a few days to recuperate. If I were my own patient, I would have prescribed a few days of rest and modified work duties. But I was too stubborn and desperate. Lack of money drove my actions. My practice was indeed a losing proposition at that time; although I had been steadily building a patient base and working long hours to do so.

The straw that finally 'broke' my back happened after a fairly typical day of treating patients. After adjusting one of my patients, I felt a pop and a pain that let me know that my body was done; I was finished. I turned the lights off at the office, rode the subway home and laid down on my back, where I remained—paralyzed with pain—for nine long weeks.

My offices were packed up and I lost the patient base that I had worked so hard to get. The pain I felt in my back was unbearable at times, with a radiating throb and burning that went all the way down the back of my thigh and into my foot.

I was distraught and extremely anxious about my situation. I couldn't believe what was happening to me. I tried to do something about my situation. I started making various appointments with all sorts of therapists and doctors. Getting around was an ordeal, but I made the effort to walk when I could. I tried many different forms of therapy: anti-inflammatory medication, traditional chiropractic adjustments, low-level laser, interferential current, lumbar traction, acupuncture and massage therapy. The different forms of therapy were somewhat helpful in dulling the pain, but it never entirely went away. I was grateful for all the help my colleagues, various doctors and therapists provided me with. I knew that they wanted me to get better and that they were doing everything they could to bring me relief. I began to question why nothing was working. Why was this happening? What had I done to deserve this? My reality was setting in and I was feeling very depressed about what my life had become.

Although I was in agony, I felt that I had to get back to work. Being at home all day gave me too much time to worry and get really anxious. At some point, I realized that I couldn't continue my work as I had done in the past. My body was revolting against me; but what was I to do? I'd invested so much time and money to go to university and then to Chiropractic College. What if I wasn't going to be able to do what I was trained to do? Fear enveloped me; I felt stunned and completely disabled. I might never work again, let alone as a chiropractor. I couldn't sit, stand or put my shoes on; I couldn't go to the movies, hang out with friends, enjoy a meal or any of the normal activities that most people take for granted.

At about that time, I had reacquainted myself with a friend and colleague who had graduated a year ahead of me. I told her of my situation and she suggested that I try something a little different. She used a few chiropractic techniques that I had heard about, but had been very doubtful of. When applied to my own situation, however, I decided I had very little to lose.

When I arrived at my friend's office, we talked about the role of stress on the body, as well as the fact that pain that lasts a long time is often not just a mechanical problem. A mechanical issue is something that arises from an area that may have been strained or sprained; like injuring an ankle while running. Typically, these injuries may be around for a few days or a week, then rapidly heal and cease to be an issue. Sometimes, other stressors can affect the rate of healing and cause the pain to last far longer.

Realizing that my problem may not be strictly physical made me think about my past and the stress I had growing up. At a very young age, I knew that my father had a drinking problem. I had done my own detective work and kept track of the level of liquor consumed from various bottles around the house. The moodiness, violent temper, apathy and absence from family gatherings were obvious signs of a problem to me; even as a young girl. As time went on, the situation grew worse, but my mother continued to work hard; ensuring there was always food on the table and that we were well taken care of. My mother never denied us her time. She encouraged us to be active in sports and drove us to our various track meets and soccer games; all while working full time, running the household and dealing with my father, who was becoming more difficult. I have always been thankful for my mother's strong will and her dedication toward my brother and I. Before I graduated from Chiropractic College, I changed my surname to Durickovic to honour her.

Money wasn't much of an issue until I was in my teens. We lived in a beautiful house in the country that my family had custom built. Financially, everything seemed fine until my mother began having difficulty paying the bills and discovered that my father had been siphoning money into a secret account.

My brother was a gifted athlete, so when he was offered a full cross-country running scholarship to Georgia State University, he leapt at the chance to get away. Once my tall, imposing brother was gone, my father had ample opportunity to become even more verbally and physically abusive toward my mother. Looking back, I can appreciate that my own issues surrounding money, security and independence were shaped by my early circumstances.

I'd always wondered if my past might somehow come back to affect me. I'd thought that I had handled things really well; only a few friends had known what was happening at home and to all outward appearances, I'd had a normal home life. But, I realized what I had been feeling inside was very different. I often had difficulty sleeping and constantly felt a low level of anxiety or tension; as if something bad was going to happen at any moment.

I began undergoing sessions of chiropractic and craniosacral therapy

(CST) and a few months later, when my friend sold the practice, the new owner continued to help me. She used another technique called Network Spinal Analysis (NSA). Truth be told, I thought it was a bizarre technique. It involved applying light pressure to areas on my spine. I was entirely skeptical as to how this was going to make me feel better. I was used to making joints pop and getting my own muscles kneaded to bring some relief. I was very hesitant, but I had tried everything else without success.

To my surprise, slowly but surely, I began to notice a change; an improvement that continued in the right direction. I also began a mindfulness meditation class that required me to meditate for an hour a day and attend a three-hour class once a week. I began to live more in the moment; to accept the pain, go into the pain, feel every bit of it and accept my circumstances just as they were, without trying to change them. I started to do more walking and gentle stretching; I even started going to the pool with Mark. I remember getting into the pool, wondering what I was doing there, as I watched everyone swim back and forth. I discovered pool noodles and flutter boards and under the tutelage of an elderly woman who frequented the pool, I slowly began making it across the pool; one length at a time.

At about the same time, the new owner of the clinic was looking for an associate and she asked me if I wanted to come on board. The offer seemed bizarre to me as I was still in a lot of pain. My old instincts for money kicked in, but I also felt compelled to begin working there; for reasons I didn't fully understand. What she was doing was helping and I needed to look a little more closely at what this was all about.

I started working a few hours a day, using a few of the less body intensive techniques that I already knew. I booked 30-minute breaks between patients so that I could lie on the table to reduce my pain and continue working. I didn't tell any of the patients, of course; I wanted to make sure that their visit to the office was about them, not me. It was an insane task, but something told me that I had to do it. I continued with my NSA sessions and mediation; living moment by moment.

After a few months of working at the clinic, I began learning some new chiropractic techniques and took an NSA seminar. I learned how the nervous system plays a vital role in running the body and that stress can accumulate in the body and nervous system, causing discomfort, pain and other symptoms. This form of chiropractic technique reduces tension in the nervous system, brings awareness to individuals and helps them connect and merge with the stress that is ultimately causing the spinal tension. This enables the individual to seek out appropriate outlets to change their perception of stress or eliminate what *they* perceive as the ultimate root cause. These individuals can then seek out other health professionals; a naturopath to help determine food sensitivities, a psychotherapist to help sort through emotional stress or even personal trainer to help them get back into physical shape and strengthen certain muscle groups. The main premise being that you know yourself best and the answers that you require about your health and how you should live lie within.

    I began to realize, thorough my own process, that the more I resisted and the more I tried to make the pain go away, the stronger it became. As I began to focus in the area of mind-body integration, my pain began to dissipate. When I became more aware of my body and conscious of the circumstances leading to pain, I felt more at ease and less fearful. When I began to let go of the hurt of the past and live moment by moment, new opportunities began presenting themselves to me. I realized that my own pain was my fuel for change. I am now grateful that I fully experienced my pain and used it; not so that I could be the person I was before I developed the pain, but someone who has evolved and developed into the person that I was intended to be.

    I began to see patients in a new light. When I talked about the role of stress and pain in their body and when they began to learn how to attain this level of awareness, I began to see some amazing things. I help people develop awareness; to understand that their mind, thoughts, emotions and stress have a powerful role in their physiology and can ultimately cause pain, discomfort and other symptoms. For example, you can become embarrassed over a comment that someone made and your face becomes red. This is an example of how a thought or emotion can change your physiology and show up physically, as redness. You may have recurring headaches on a daily basis, which respond well to various forms of treatment, but never really go away. If you gain the awareness that you hold tension in your upper back and neck because you're always angry, you can begin to work on the ultimate cause of the pain, which is the anger and the issues and circumstances that have created this reality for you. This is true healing.

My journey to get beyond 'why me?' took a few years. When I was injured, I felt like a victim; like there was no way out of what I was experiencing. I've realized that I can't think like a victim; I have to get up and do something about it. The approach I was taking wasn't working and I couldn't keep doing the same thing over again; expecting a different result to emerge. I needed to go beyond my conventional thinking and leave behind preconceived notions about what healthcare and healing were supposed to be about. Now, getting on my feet (literally and figuratively), I've discovered that my role isn't only to treat people, but also to help them understand that they don't need to be victims. I help patients get past their own 'why me?' moments in their lives.

People who feel like victims; whether because of physical pain or their life circumstances, need to keep exploring their options. Many individuals have preconceived notions about what is right or real and limit their choices to those things that fit nicely into that illusion. There is always more that can be done or learned and it often begins by looking within. There is a solution out there, even if you have been told that there isn't. You just need to break down the barriers of your own thinking and discover it. This isn't a journey that you need to take alone. People like me can help you move beyond feeling like a victim. It's not about popping a pill and hoping that it goes away; it's about changing your mindset, using your own pain as your fuel for change and living up to your full potential.

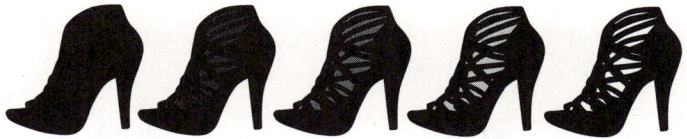

Larissa Gomes

I love heels. Platforms, stilettos, even those oddly named 'kitten' heels. They have given me a much broader perspective; literally... I'm only 5'3" tall. I wore high heels precociously, as a little girl playing dress up; I wore them, awkwardly, as a teenager trying to get into clubs and I wear them, lovingly and often, as an adult, whenever I feel like it. I think I look fine in flats or sneakers, to be honest; but as a woman in the entertainment business, a good pair of high heels is a wardrobe must-have in your tote, carry-on or car trunk!

Looking back, it wasn't the heels that got me through my struggles, but they sure made me feel a lot more graceful making it. Here's how it started.

Mom's 80's heels were much too big for me as a child, yet I still managed to make my way downstairs to the dinner table in those snakeskin fire engine red pumps with gold trim! Yikes. We practically have the same shoe size now, but even with all the 80's retro fashion madness going on, those ones are thankfully buried forever!

As a child, I could observe people for hours. I'd watch their revealing gestures and intuit their desires and motivations. Imagining their lives was endlessly fascinating to me. I used to think I was different from everyone else. However, now that I can see the bigger picture, I know that was only the seed that sparked the passion I have developed as an actor. Back then, my only outlet was 'directing' and 'performing' little shows that all my parents' friend's kids would put on at the big New Year's party; whether the parents liked it or not. I would often walk up to complete strangers who appeared sad, on the street, bus or park bench, and ask them why were they so blue. My mother would promptly apologize and pull me away from them. But, somehow I recognized and identified with their sadness; it drew me in. Maybe it was just catholic school guilt!

I was a shy girl in grade school, but I found comfort in drama, art and music. I'd routinely sit in front of the mirror making faces and imitating the laughs, facial expressions and mannerisms of others. Rarely did a conversation with my family end without a funny face or characterization of one of their friends' accents or one of my teachers' mannerisms. Much to my sister and mother's annoyance, (although they laughed, hopefully with me and not at me), I was always genuinely fueled on by my father, who could be sillier than me as a six year old!

Musically, I played the French horn in my grade school band, I know; booooring. I was late for school that day and it was the only instrument left. My music teacher, Madame Murray (I went to a French school), told me it was the hardest instrument to master (a little helpful white lie, I'm sure) and that if I could play that; I could do anything. So, by appealing to the side of me that wants to be able to do anything, my teacher taught me to love that instrument almost as much as I loved grilled cheese sandwiches. I played it with everything I had.

In high school, I performed in plays as a matter of course. I felt it was a necessary art; not only as a student and performer, but as a developing adult. Drama became a welcome form of expression for my angst and rebellion. That rebellion, unfortunately, also found a home in partying and all the other clichéd forms of teenage experience. I'll spare you the details; if only so that my parents don't have to relive the moments in which their loving daughter morphed into a monster alien being with a penchant toward profanity. I excelled, however (in an average way) at school, despite my tendencies and art became a favorite subject for me; especially after witnessing my 10th grade math teacher have a massive mental breakdown in class and have to be escorted out by the principal. Not fun. I often think of her, I hope she is okay today.

However, during my university career, I strayed from drama and theatre and concentrated mainly on my major, Sociology. I leaned toward the study of criminology, and imagined a 'safe' yet still exciting career in criminal law. It should have been a no-brainer, really; so many family members are doctors, lawyers or engineers and acting wasn't exactly a career thought to have enough stability to build a future on. However, I am the first in the family to pursue it. I enjoyed school because I was learning so much; but I knew in my gut, something was missing for me. I examined my choices; I could see the reasons behind choosing Sociology as my course of study in school. Here, I had the study of social groups; how one's environment and perspective can affect behavior in relationships on a micro level and macro level. I had still found a way to fulfill my real interests; the study of the human condition. This is what drew me to storytelling and acting in the first place.

I had never relinquished my love of music, poetry and songwriting throughout my studies; during university I sang in several soul/ funk bands. I was a member of a pop/R&B group in Atlanta, Georgia, by the name of *MiLaDi*. It was an exciting time for me; I traveled to Atlanta, during time off from school and we recorded in the same studios as *TLC*. We managed to land a deal that unfortunately (or fortunately) never took off.

This was due in large part to the wise words of my entertainment lawyer, who advised me to run as far away from the situation as possible. He had taken a good look at the contract, which was heavily slanted toward the interests of everyone but the artists. The contract's fine print would have had us giving up most of our rights and hard earned royalties. I learned a lot! Always double-check contracts and hire a good representative.

Upon university graduation, I was looking for a break from so much schooling and a way to pay for it all. One day, I received a call from an old band member. He asked me if I would be interested in auditioning for a cover band set to play in a five star hotel for six months in Hong Kong. I jumped at the chance; more for the experience of living abroad and the training I would surely get by singing six nights a week for four hours. Of course, living in a five star hotel was a bit of a factor in my decision. Hello room service and very, very nice to meet you, housekeeping! After years of being a starving student, it was like a dream come true.

Everything was going extremely well and some of the members of the band were exceedingly talented and experienced; from which I learned a lot. I thrived in my new environment and culture as I sharpened my skills.

However, four and half months in, the other female singer in the band and I were 'warned' by hotel management that we were to dress in a more revealing style. We laughed at the suggestion and continued about our business; only to receive a notice of termination if we should not comply. This was ridiculous! It was blatant sexual discrimination and we didn't stand for it.

Eventually, we found out that the hotel, not doing as well financially as they had hoped that quarter, had hired a hatchet man to come in and cut costs. As the mere singers in the band, we were considered disposable; they could do with an instrumental band for the last end of the contract's run. This of course, was a complete breach of contract which stipulated that we were entitled to 30 days notice of termination or payment thereof in lieu of notice; none of which we received. We were told to leave quietly the next day! I don't do well with unfair treatment and resolved to show them just who they were dealing with.

So, we decided to contact the Canadian consulate. They weren't able help to us as we were in a 'three tier' private work contract. On to the labor board for obvious breach of contract; we were told it would take months to come to a resolution. So, last but not least, we visited the Equal Opportunity Commission. They immediately took our case as an illegal form of discrimination. To further make our voices heard, we arranged an interview with a writer I'd met at the *South China Morning Post*, who ran our story the next day. I didn't realize at the time what a big deal the whole situation would become. There hadn't been a case like that since shorter hemlines in the office caused a big stir, five years prior. I stayed in Hong Kong for a few more months, working with another band and fighting the case. However, I was homesick and knew I couldn't stay much longer. In the end, we never received the money we were owed, but I was proud to have set an example for other women in similar situations. It would have been far worse to feel that I hadn't done everything in my power to be heard in the face of injustice.

Back home again, I was encouraged to consider music as a full time career. I thought I might be interested in musical theatre, since I enjoyed performing on stage so much. I set out to acquire an agent as soon as I returned to Toronto. I joined an acting class that offered a broad, integrated knowledge of most acting techniques; borrowing some of the best ideas from classical acting methods. It was important for me to study the basics and to observe my 'learned' habits on camera. If I was to give film and television a shot, I needed to be able to start a character with a clean slate. The advice I received from peers and teachers was a great strengthening experience before I set out into the world of massive amounts of rejection. I took more classes, scene study, commercial technique, improvisation and theatre studies. I also joined on as one of the leads in the cast of a musical play. I dropped off flyers for that show to gain access to agents, to show them that I wasn't just sitting around, waiting for something to happen to me. In terms of doing what you can to stay fresh while not taking classes, I have something I still do to this day…I let music on the radio move me to tears while driving, to practice my emotional readiness. I realize what I must look like to other drivers; who are probably wishing I had invested in tinted windows!

I found an agency and the right agent; everything clicked. I followed my gut instinct and I was right to do so, because I am still with her today. My first film audition was for a movie opposite *Eric Roberts*. I was to play a Puerto-Rican girl from the Bronx. I studied the accent and made that character as real as I imagined her to be. The casting director took a chance on me; considering that I was an unknown with no track record. I believe they wanted me for the role. It was a lead in a film, though and because of my inexperience, I was told it was too big a gamble for producers to take on. I was ecstatic, however. The whole experience confirmed my feeling that I was ready and should continue to "pay my dues."

The following year opened doors to many more casting directors in Toronto and one-liner parts soon led to five lines; which led to nine lines and so on. I was a working actor and it felt fantastic! I was living a dream and making a decent living at it; I felt so lucky. I shot commercials and small roles on television and then I got a break. In an amazing turn of events, a one-episode role I did for a series called "*La Femme Nikita*" was extended and I became a regular character on the series during the last season. It was such an amazing experience to be part of a show and really get to know the people I worked with.

Over the next few years, I worked steadily; some years more than others, but enough overall to see a significant retirement savings building up with my union. I worked for prime time networks, as well as cable. The industry was booming in Toronto; before SARS changed the landscape.

I was also a dancer, constantly taking dance classes to stay somewhat trained. I booked work in films and television on dance crews. It was mainly hip-hop dance, but I also learned ballroom dancing and the tango for different projects. That was a fun and exciting challenge! As an actor, it's important to keep training both your voice and body.

Because I come from a multi-cultural, multi-ethnic background, my look or 'hit category' was varied. My exposure to a multitude of cultures growing up in Toronto has given me a rich landscape to draw from. I've worked in a broad range of ethnicities from South American to Egyptian, Italian, Greek, French, Indian, Middle-Eastern and British (yes, British). Although I portray mainly characters with some visible ethnicity, casting has never truly been able to pinpoint a specific look for me in terms of stereotyping. I've found that there isn't as much representation in ethnic roles, so I tended to work less in the past, but I've noticed that an ethnically ambiguous look is becoming more commonplace and thankfully, the previously rigid rules regarding casting seem to be relaxing somewhat. It's important to know what my 'hit category' is, but I would never allow that to narrow my scope as a performer. I can do anything to transform myself for a character; it's one of the skills actors have.

If only the relaxing of casting rules could extend into the age category. One can't play 'ingénue' (teens and early 20's) forever. Truth be told, we value youth almost viciously in this culture and although ageism is a truism in this business, I can only hope for the day that multi dimensional roles are written for women of all ages. Nowadays, cable networks routinely portray female centered shows and I'd say the future looks much brighter.

We now come to the part of my story where the heels, well, break. I came to be 'hip-pocketed' (not officially represented) by *Paradigm*, a large LA agency, during 'pilot season' (casting and shooting of pilot television projects occurs from January through April) at the time of some hype I had surrounding a film. My first foray into the world of Hollywood casting was a bit overwhelming. I had to navigate new territory, find a place to live and spend all my hard earned money just to survive. I found myself couch surfing, car pooling and dipping dangerously into my credit cards during my first few trips to Los Angeles.

Sitting in the waiting room for an audition with actresses I had seen and admired for years on some of my favorite films and shows, was very inspiring. On the other hand, listening to some 20 year olds complain about how fat their ankles were and how much they needed Botox and diuretics; not so much! Los Angeles can be a contradiction; at once beautiful landscapes, motivating, positive energy and full of creative dreamers and then sometimes vain, desperate, callous and insincere. I had to come to terms with what it is and eventually I found like minded people and the very unique terrain that Los Angeles has to offer became more manageable and even, believe it or not, enjoyable.

I tried to return for another pilot season in 2002, but things didn't go exactly as planned. I was over my head in expenses and without a legal work visa, I couldn't cut it. I returned to Toronto, where I continued happily to work in my field. I was no longer attached to the agency in Los Angeles and had to start all over again. I skipped a year and returned in 2004 to procure representation. I did. However, it took months and by that time, pilot season was already over. So, I returned and settled in for pilot season 2005.

Two weeks into it, I got my big break! I landed a series regular part in a pilot for *ABC*. I shot the pilot for three weeks, with *Kyle MacLachlan* and other amazing actors. I played a young lawyer in a role that felt tailor made for me. She was an idealistic crusader for justice and I had studied criminology…ok, well, I imagined it was tailor made for me. The show was called *In Justice*. It was about a group of eager, young lawyers, paired with detectives who worked with the D.A. in an attempt to overturn the convictions of innocent people on death row. It was a great pilot; it was so well written that I felt an instant connection with the material. It was shot incredibly well and it had a serious, gripping subject matter.

The news got even better when the announcement came that the pilot had been picked up! It was going to air in the fall or mid-season and we would shoot at least 13 episodes. Hallelujah! I would be able to move out on my own and actually furnish the place without the help of second hand stores. I attended my first 'Upfronts' in New York (this is where the networks throw a red carpet gala to announce the season's shows to advertisers). It was such a rush; the red carpet, the press, the parties. I loved every minute of it. I had my best heels on!

Then one day, my manager called to tell me they had replaced my role with another character, someone older (in Hollywood? Now THAT is odd), in order to be a love interest to the detective I was paired with. Well, I was disappointed; to say the least. I was having lunch in a restaurant when I got the news and I quickly put my sunglasses on as tears gathered and I heard my friend order, "two shots of tequila, right away, please!"

I had my doubts as to whether that was in fact the reason for my replacement, as I knew that politics are alive and well in any business and development deals regularly have actors moving from one show to another. I can speculate, but in the end, it's not going to do any good. I had lost the role I already had. It can happen; it did happen. But I was grateful for the experience and I just kept on pushing!

Now, I was armed, I had opened doors as a lead actor for myself in Hollywood and I had a three year visa which allowed me to work. It was a win-win situation, if you ask me. I worked on a few other projects and I was even beginning to have some luck with some screen-writing opportunities. I had optioned a script I co-wrote and it was being shopped by an agent at William Morris. However, nothing is a guarantee in this business and the script was relegated to a backburner. That hasn't slowed me down, though; I co-wrote a television pilot and a few other scripts that garnered some interest. I will continue to do so, until something happens.

In late 2005, tragedy struck and brought my momentum to a stand still. Following an unimaginable tragedy, the murder of a friend and some other personal issues that emerged, I returned to Toronto to stay with family and spent a year and a half healing and writing.

I was back in Los Angeles by the summer of 2007 with my heels back on once again. Almost immediately, I was offered a lead role in a television movie; it fell through because I had chopped all my hair off. They had offered me the role based on my reel and a referral and unfortunately, the producer providing the bulk of financial backing for the project was inflexible. His lead actress had to have long hair and wearing extensions or a wig wouldn't be acceptable; it was a period piece involving a lot of horseback riding that would be shot in the hot desert. I can't help but wonder; if I were *Angelina Jolie*, would that have made a difference? The answer to that is, absolutely. It was another small setback.

However, I was ready to get back to work. I was short listed for a series regular in a fabulous pilot; then…the infamous writer's strike, well, struck. That pilot project became one of many of the time that was shelved and more than likely, buried.

There are going to be highs and lows in any career; sometimes due to personal reasons, sometimes for reasons completely out of one's control. It will be tough and challenging and developing the coping skills required to stick it out will be necessary if I am to keep my belief in myself.

I traveled to Goa, India during the strike and enjoyed experiencing the culture; I took photos and became inspired again to think beyond the short term setbacks. I have many interests and dreams for the future and so many inspirations on a daily basis. As long as I maintain the consciousness my experience has afforded me and stay open to new opportunities, my creative force is limitless. I have been back at creating music; writing songs for other artists, as well as compiling my own album. I have found great new motivation to write a book. In 2008, in the wake of the writer's strike and the looming actor's strike, the industry's playing field has fundamentally changed on some level. Now, in 2009, things seem to have settled and I am gratefully acting, writing and producing/creating projects. Armed with the knowledge I have acquired over the years; balance is, in fact, the key to all successful pursuits. So, I still have my heels on and I know I have a much more balanced gait. I think now, however, I'll add some cleats. I hear *Dolce and Gabbana* make a fabulous pair!

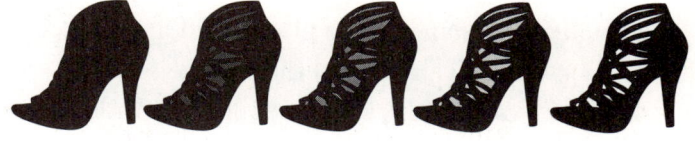

Lynn Manwar

In November 1996, I graduated from university and at the tender age of 23, I was ready to get started in the world and make my dreams a reality. Less than a week later, I sat in my thyroid specialist's office and was told I could possibly have cancer. My sense of accomplishment in completing a post-secondary education was clouded over by an uncertain future. Of course, I thought it was nothing. After all, I was a young woman and young people aren't supposed to get cancer.

Despite the uncertainty that lay ahead, I decided to move forward and applied for a teaching job in Japan. It had been my goal to work and live overseas after university. In March 1997, while applying for the job, I underwent surgery and half of my thyroid and two nodules were removed. Shortly after my hospital stay, I received a job offer to work in Nagano, Japan to teach high school students and volunteers for the upcoming Olympic Winter Games. I gladly accepted the position.

Just a few weeks later, I returned to my surgeon's office to get my test and surgery results. I'll never forget that day in early April 1997, when the surgeon told me, "You have cancer and we will have to operate again." That was the most devastating news of my life. I left my doctor's office that day crying, with my dream of going to Japan shattered. I worried that I was going to die, but for a split second, I was more upset that I might not be able to go to Japan anymore.

In May 1997, my total thyroidectomy was completed with the removal of three more cancerous nodules. Everyone around me advised me to cancel my plans to work and live in Japan; including close friends and members of my family. There were only two people who believed in me—my father and a male friend; both who said, "You can do it." They gave me hope when I didn't have any.

My battle wasn't over and I was scheduled for radioactive iodine treatment for the overkill of any remaining cancer cells left in my body. This type of treatment involved ingesting three radioactive pills and being in isolation in the hospital for several days. I gained a new resolve while in isolation. I visualized myself finishing a year in Japan and receiving an expression of thanks from my future employer. Three weeks later, with the treatment finished, I flew out to Nagano, Japan.

The Opening Ceremonies of the 1998 Nagano Winter Olympic Games showed me peace at it's finest, with people from all around the world, from numerous backgrounds and speaking many different languages joined together for the common goal of sport and cultural understanding. This was followed by a visit to Hiroshima, Japan, where I witnessed the devastation war can have on a society and its people.

Cancer was one of my first great teachers. I learned that when you fear cancer, it controls you; but when you embrace cancer, it sets you free. Anything is possible.

A few years after my return from Japan, my recruiting career began. I was eager to take on a new challenge and was successful at establishing myself in the recruitment industry.

The year 2003 rolled around and my five year streak of a clean bill of health was shattered as I started to walk with a limp and had ongoing swelling of my left leg. I visited a health clinic and was told of the possibility that I had arthritis, which to me was an old person's disease. That simply couldn't happen to me; or so I thought.

With my usual socializing and volunteering, I had spent the previous night at a South Asian Gala in late September 2003. The next morning, when I awoke in my bed, I found to my surprise, that I had body pain and swollen joints all over; I couldn't get out of bed. I didn't know it at the time, but I was experiencing my first taste of an arthritic 'flare-up.' More 'flare-ups' were to follow with my diagnosis of Psoriatic Arthritis at the age of 30.

Physical challenges threatened to overwhelm my life and performing everyday tasks were proving extremely difficult. Opening jars, turning doorknobs, washing dishes and even going to the toilet seemed like insurmountable tasks. I had to figure out how to cope with this new body of mine and continue to lead a normal life as an independent young lady.

I was going through the motions at work in my position as a recruiter; I had lost the drive to 'wheel and deal' as I was in so much pain. I took on the challenge of researching my illness and doing everything in my power to lead a full life with arthritis. I bought a jar opener, a raised toilet seat and asked others to open my bottled water when out in public. I learned how to be self-sufficient, but I needed something more. Being self-sufficient was one thing, but being healthy was an entirely different game to play.

With the support of my family, in November 2003, I submitted my resignation to my employer. I recall phoning my friend, novelist and ascension expert Andrea Hansen, the next day, and she said, "Congratulations on resigning from your job! Get ready to have the time of your life." I thought, "Congratulations??? What, are you crazy? I've just left a great career behind." What I thought was the biggest misfortune of my life, turned out to be a blessing in disguise and an adventure unimaginable.

The recruitment skills I had acquired in the employment agency were transferable. In 2004, I began my next career as a Volunteer Coordinator and recruited and coordinated volunteers for six festivals dealing with 50 to 600 plus volunteers per festival. What had seemed to be a misfortune turned into a career of fun. Working in the arts allowed creativity and passion into my life. "Congratulations...."--- boy, Andrea was right! Passion is needed in everyone's work life. I had to get arthritis to realize that.

In April 2006, I sat in the audience of my monthly mentor program, where participants wrote their monthly goals and shared their successes. I recall listening to one participant who had just recently undergone an image makeover. I secretly wished I could have a makeover. Two weeks later, on a Saturday morning, I was approached at St. Lawrence Market by a stranger who gave me a card and asked me to send in a few digital photos of myself to the TV show she worked for. It was *Style by Jury*, looking to cast people who were in dire need of a makeover. She must have thought I looked really bad that day. Nothing became of that chance encounter, though; I didn't have a digital camera and never sent in any photos.

That summer, I had made note of my monthly goal to have an image makeover as part of my mentor program. Several months later, when my aunt saw me dressed to go out for dinner, she blurted, "You look like crap." Those words were a wake up call for me and a few days later, I was surfing the net and came across an ad to become a candidate for a makeover show called, *Style by Jury*. I was crossing paths once again with the same television show. I applied for and got an audition.

The big day for the audition came and I met the host, Bruce Turner. I had never seen the show before, as I don't have cable television, so during the audition, I got the surprise of my life! The 'Style Jury' was behind a two-way mirror and they had been watching me all along. I wasn't auditioning. I was already a makeover candidate and the process had already begun.

My encounter with the jury exposed a woman dressed in baggy tops and pants and granny shoes, with skin on my arms that was dry and scaly. My teeth were stained and I had more gum than tooth showing when I smiled. My hair was long and shapeless and my old, round eyeglasses did nothing to complement my face.

The jury commented on the first impressions I had made and I had to admit; some of the comments were hard to hear. One juror felt that I was using my arthritis as a crutch: "She seems to be defining herself through her arthritis and using it as an excuse for the way she looks." Many of the comments had some truth to them and after the jury session, I was invited by Bruce to spend the next seven days getting a makeover with a team of experts.

The makeover journey involved a transformation about how I felt about myself and how I looked. Four years previous, I had been diagnosed with arthritis. To help me deal with the psychological and physical barriers that I had acquired with this disease, I had a few meetings with a life coach. The coach picked up that I defined myself by what 'I can't do,' rather than what 'I can do.' The transformation of my feelings about myself involved taking on more risk and injecting passion into my life and essentially, stepping out of my comfort zone.

Along with the reality TV show, my life coach presented me with a surprise challenge. I, along with the film crew, ended up at the *Toronto School of Circus Arts*. My task was to climb the ladder to the trapeze and swing away. When I got there, the thought of having to climb a ladder and support myself on a trapeze scared me. For starters, my hands have lost much of their grip due to the arthritis. Some days, just walking up the stairs is a challenge for me; I had my doubts about climbing up a ladder. The host of the TV show and my life coach gently reminded me of the mantra, "I can do it." With much hesitation and a few stops along the ladder, I got up there and took the plunge and swung away with the trapeze. It was both a scary and exhilarating moment for me. As I landed in the safety net, tears flowed down my cheeks. I cried tears of joy; it was a liberating moment in my life. I realized and adopted the mindset of "I can do it." My mind had fueled my body with the strength that it needed.

Writing monthly goals is a habit I continued into the spring of 2008 and I wrote that I wanted to eat healthier meals one day. Shortly thereafter, I attracted a raw food coach into my life. I received free coaching and support and started an internal body transformation. I adopted new patterns of thinking and relating to food. My shopping habits evolved and fruits and plant foods became my new allies. The changes I noticed were subtle, but life impacting. I was no longer on my arthritis medication and more importantly, my knee pain disappeared.

The other miracle happened when I had a double lumpectomy on my left breast on May 21st, 2008. The surgeon had been concerned that it could have been cancer, but miraculously on June 9th, 2008, the reports came back negative! Raw foods had done my body good!

My road to recovery hasn't been an easy one. There were many times when I felt like giving up; countless days that I cried my eyes out and asked, "Why me?" Then I learned the question, "Why not me?" My twelve years of health challenges and eventual triumphs, have made me into the woman I am today. I've learned that anything is possible, the importance of passion and that I can do it; whatever it is. I live life to the fullest and I am doing everything I desire.

I have accomplished many things so far and achieved most of the goals I've set for myself. I finished university, traveled to many countries in the world, lived on my own, started a business, invested my money and purchased real estate. Life is an ever winding road of growth and more lies ahead in my future.

The keys to achieving one's goals are simple. Write them down and share your super achievements-to-be with everyone you meet. Act as if the goal is already completed; own the outcome.

My future goals include having a family, developing and expanding my business, more traveling, contributing to society and helping make the world a better place. A goal is just one component of bringing dreams to reality. The qualities of a person make goals happen. I bring to the table possibility, vision, passion, belief, integrity and action. I treat my word as gold and the world around me becomes golden---auto-magically!

Jade Anthony

In 1979, a young Indian woman named Palmjet gave birth to Jade Martine Cheema in England. The birth of her first child should have been a joyous occasion for Palmjet, but as a seventeen-year-old single mother, it was anything but. Having been disowned by her family for becoming pregnant by a 'Jack-the-Lad' English boy, Palmjet was left with no option but to have me adopted. This was the beginning of my life…

Adoption was not a decision my birth mother came to lightly; on three occasions within the first six months of my life, she tried to regain custody of me. The tug-of-war was put to rest by my adopted parents, who took a firm stand with Palmjet. With no real means to support herself and no family support, Palmjet realized she couldn't offer the stable and loving environment they could offer; she allowed Beverley and Christopher to become my new parents and I became Jade Rebecca Anthony.

By the time I was four, my parents had also adopted a boy named Thomas and we had relocated to a nearby town, Ashford. It was great having a younger brother; someone I could annoy and play with. But, I have to say, we had a very love-hate relationship, at times. We just didn't understand each other. We were both told we were adopted from a young age, but were given so much love and honesty that I never saw it as a problem. However, in my later years, I realized that it may have been a factor with some of the issues I dealt with growing up.

My childhood was rich with religion, music, great family times, fun, laughter, guides and Brownies; all of which provided me with a great outlook on life that I later realized a lot of other people may not have had. Although my upbringing was great and fruitful with love, we were not well off like others in our area and at times, there were many things that we couldn't afford. That's not to say that those richer than us were any better off; many never received love and weren't encouraged to develop their skills and talents the way they would have liked.

I learned to play the violin at the age of eleven and had been singing in choirs and with my mum from the age of seven. This was a great boost for my self-confidence and gave me a passion for the stage; as a result, I constantly crave the attention of others, whether good or bad.

Throughout my childhood, I dreamt of winning an Oscar and having a number one hit record. I was attracted to being recognized for my talents and achievements, the fabulous lifestyle and the idea of having a platform to be able to reach out to people. I truly believed I had the talent to succeed. But, looking back, I think my motivation might have been a bit of 'fuck you' toward my birth parents; I wanted to prove that I could achieve success and that I am a special and worthy person.

I remember being certain that I was destined to be *Supermodel of Great Britain* and dragging my poor Nan to the competition. That day was eventful, to say the least; not only had I made it through to the finals, but I ended up winning *Lou Lou Girl* of the Year, which was a competition for the finalists of the *Supermodel of Great Britain*.

With my Nan in tow, we wooed the judges; or rather my Nan did. Toward the end of the day, I caught her holding court with all the famous male models of the 90's and *The Chippendales,* too. They were all hanging off her every word. For me, that was the best day of my life. Not only had my Nan charmed the managers of the event, the models and TV personalities, but she had also managed to attract the world's leading male strip tease troupe, who sung for her personally! That, my friends, is girl power at 70.

High school passed quickly and after an amazing summer spent discovering a spiritual connection to America, I was off to college to study Performing Arts. It was my dream, but in spite of that, I struggled with the workload and my mind just kept wandering all over the place. I wanted to be in one of the great cities such as New York or London, trying to make it as a model or even working in PR and that would then allow me to possibly achieve my music dream. I kept thinking that maybe I needed to be abroad to do this and instead, I found myself sitting in the college canteen one day, wondering what I was doing there; who I was and where I intended to go in my life. To make matters worse, I had a great part time job and was earning excellent money and I had just started a seeing a guy I really liked. Rather than persevere with the hard work of studying, I began to socialize with many friends and soon found myself in a crowd that consisted of a load of bored students, wanting to party it up every weekend; taking drugs, drinking and living carefree with no concerns for their future or studies. I knew that I had the looks and personality to get the lucky break I needed; it was just a matter of when, not if.

One day, after a crazy argument with my mother, she packed me off to a bedsit that she had found me in the middle of town; I was to learn to live life on my own, without affecting family life so adversely. I was feeling stuck in that quiet, small town

Almost as soon as I had moved into the bedsit, I dropped out of college. I was no longer in a position to sit back and let Mum and Dad pay the bills; suddenly I had to pay for food, rent, utilities and a social life that at that time was very important to me. I found myself in a whirlwind of work, parties and good times. I spent many hours throughout the day wondering whether I would have been better off living at my parents and continuing with my studies. But no, I thought, 'fuck it,' this is about life experience and nothing could have taught me many of the things I was about to learn through the next couple of years.

But, of course, the path I chose was a rocky one, indeed; resulting in many depressive episodes of hanging out with friends that had no care for my dreams, but thought only of parties and more parties. At the tender age of 18, I found myself broke, in debt, suffering from depression and on benefits. Suddenly the dream had become just a dream. There were no big paychecks, no satisfaction of achievement, no family and friends in admiration and no abundance. There was just one big mess; all because I had allowed myself to take a journey into the unknown and away from the safety and security of family life and education.

In those darkest hours, I probably had met the most interesting and spiritual people from many different backgrounds; even many with decent jobs and normal home lives. Yet they all appeared to have the same reality: to party, party, party. Many of those people would go home at the end of the night to their home comforts and 9–5 jobs. Was that the life I really wanted?

I certainly had no joy in finding a job, let alone keeping one. I was constantly starting jobs, only to quit or get fired. I was a disgrace to myself and my family; I had no idea how to function in the real world. Yet, being on the dole, I thought I was functioning all right.

I'd wake up, smoke a joint with a few mates and meet up with friends down the pub and share a few laughs. After work, I'd meet up with more friends, we'd come back to mine and smoke some more joints; I even let a mate sell drugs from my bed-sit. Drugs are something that are no longer in my life and something I no longer condone. My friends and I would party at the local club with no cares in the world, come back to mine with half the club, rave till morning and start it all over again. That went on five days a week for two years. I was never one to leave the party first; I thought, "This is it; this is the life until someone sees the potential in me."

I will never forget the day I sat there in darkness one night, after losing the plot and throwing all my mates out. Suddenly, the party was over and I didn't just shut the door, I slammed it. My life had become a mess and I was basically running a youth club on drugs. I knew I had to make some changes and fast or I was going to end up in jail or dying of an accidental overdose.

For the next few weeks, I set about trying to make some changes in my life. I moved into a new flat and even went to a couple of job interviews in London. But, they saw right though me; how does one explain two years out of work and college? I was a wreck and couldn't see a way out. One evening, desperate for one more night of fun, I allowed a friend who really couldn't be trusted talk me into dropping speed one more time. Within minutes, I was slumped on the floor, knowing I had made a huge mistake. After a very long night, spent hoping I wasn't about to die, I knew I had hit bottom; enough was enough.

The next day, I rang my Nan. I was a mess; I had no food and I had barely made it through the night alive. I needed to hug someone and I wanted to acknowledge the terrifyingly addictive, lonely path I had chosen; straying from my dreams. The only person I knew that would understand and give me great advice was my Nan. Nan is what you might call 'Old School,' but with the voice of an angel; reason and purity and tolerance.

As soon as Nan arrived, she immediately knew something was wrong and gave me a huge hug. I will never know how she knew how much I needed that. Nan then proceeded to insist that I move in with her and Grandad immediately.

At first, I feared for my independence, but then I realized that if my dream was real, I must put in the hard work to make it happen. From that moment, I never looked back. I stayed with my grandparents for a year and half and even worked at a local restaurant. I had finally broken through the destructive barriers of drug addiction and partying. Suddenly, I found myself eating properly, working hard, making lists of my dreams and writing down action plans. I even had the time and energy to enjoy a couple of dates and my first long term relationship. I was still in touch with all my old party friends, although contact was limited to phone chats and a couple of visits by friends that my Nan trusted.

You might be thinking that I may as well have been in rehab with all the rules. Well I was; my Nan's rehab and it was safe and warm and loving and I knew that I finally had a chance at rebuilding a good path for my future. I often wonder what would have happened to my life if it hadn't been for my Nan and I would strongly encourage anyone reading this to be open to anyone in their family who wants to help; break down those barriers and let them reach out to you. Sometimes you need love and support that you may not be able to give yourself!

A few years later, I finally met a decent and trustworthy man; we settled down and in 2001, I gave birth to a very beautiful, healthy boy, named Carlin. For the first time in my life, I felt complete. I knew from that moment on that nothing could come close to the joy and unconditional love that I felt for my son.

As many relationships tend to go these days, we started having differences of opinion and within the first few months of the birth of our son, I suddenly felt very overwhelmed by my life's decisions. I was awash in guilt and panic; questioning my decisions. Was I following my dream or had I chosen the easy option of meeting a decent man and settling down? Life is never easy and would be a struggle, no matter who or where you are; but I felt that things weren't right in both our lives and that if they weren't right for us, my son would be affected for the rest of his life. I certainly didn't want our son to go through hardships in his lifetime because of my actions. We parted ways.

I was a 21 and I was working hard at being a full time mum; I even managed to work part time. Very quickly, my ambition started coming back to me; I knew I had to achieve my dreams.

It was at this time that I also started to feel an acknowledgment of my birth mother's feelings; I began to feel almost inspired by her. Suddenly, I could empathize with the struggle to achieve personal dreams, balanced with family life and raising a child. But it was this life that wasn't going to get me where I needed to be and neither would it get our son anywhere. With a dad that had a good-paying job and a mum saddled with debt who only worked part time, what hope was there of a decent future for our son with all my debt?

So, after much agonizing consideration, in the summer of 2002, I made the choice mutually with my son's father and without interference from family or friends, to swap parental roles and for my son's father to raise our son during the week, while I would have my son at weekends and for holidays. This was frowned upon by every one of my friends and some of my family; but at the end of the day, no one has the right to judge as we made this choice to suit us both and for our son and it has been the best choice we ever made. Our son is very happy and unaffected by our choice. In fact, our son is very loving, polite and happy and has the most amazing personality.

I left my son and his belongings with his father and hopped aboard the coach to London. Looking through the window at my hometown as we drove off, I knew that as hard as the next few months would be, deep down I had made the best decision. I would come back to my home town eventually, once I had created the life I dreamt of for me and our son.

As the years went by, I worked at a variety of jobs in many different places and was still actively involved in my son's parenting; especially on weekends when he would come to stay with me. Those were my favourite times; they still are. I paid for child maintenance and managed to clear some of my debts.

With my new sense of confidence and self-esteem came the realization that my boyfriend, a music producer, was jealous, possessive and way too controlling. I'm not suggesting that he was entirely to blame, as we both made our relationship crazy through some terrible tough times we both faced; especially financially and through his work. I had thought my break had finally come when some model friends and their manager invited me to be part of a singing group; with my boyfriend producing. He was far too threatened by the prospect, however and soon sabotaged my chances. Obviously, our relationship couldn't survive under those circumstances, along with many other things that had been happening.

I was on my own again, fighting hard to stay in a job and pay my own way. In that time, I even found myself living back at my parents' house for two months to take stock of the trauma of the break-up of a relationship that had lasted six years at the cost of so much effort and energy. My stay there also gave me a chance to put right the wrongs I had committed in my past with my parents. It was a very healing time for us all and at that point, I found the flat of my dreams in London and off I went.

For the next few years, I continued to live in London and worked in many jobs; some that would have had my Nan shaking her head. London is expensive; it is reputed to be the most expensive city in the world, so it wasn't surprising that one day I trotted off to the local lap dancing bars and auditioned in several clubs. One even gave me the job, but I have to say that as much as I felt highly liberated in stripping off my clothes and putting my dancing training into action, the novelty wore off quickly. After four hours of working, I blagged severe stomach pains and rushed out with my 60 pound tips and never looked back. I even worked at a Hostess Club. The Club was an interesting experience, to say the least. The job involved chatting away to young, rich guys (some were old too, but they didn't half have some stories) and getting them to buy bottles of champagne. I could earn around 250 pounds per night. As much as I hated doing the job, it earned me money to pay my bills, rent and the upkeep of my son. Hostessing also paid for a music business that I had started.

By this time, I had a dream and I was determined to put in the hard work to make it a reality. I certainly wasn't letting anyone get in the way of my desires. I knew that at some point, I would one day meet the people that would open the door to my career and I'd finally have the last laugh.

The modeling scene at that time was saturated with eastern European girls that would work for almost nothing. I knew that running my own business would be great for me financially and eventually, I would meet the right producer.

As luck would have it and thanks to the invention of social networking sites, I got asked by a top producer to record a few house tracks. It was a great start and I will never forget the buzz of recording my vocals and putting the tunes together. This was a moment of great satisfaction for all that I had been through and I knew that I had to keep working hard at my dreams; I couldn't give up at the slightest bit of depression or dark times. After all, I had a vision to share with young people in the future and I had to prove that I could do it; no matter what the odds!

After a year, I had built great contacts, my business was going well, modeling castings were coming through and I was finally getting close to great music management. I felt that I was one step closer to building the life I desired for my son and myself.

After a terrifyingly dangerous, dark relationship with an ex that lasted four months; long enough for red flags to go up, but short enough to walk away, I decided to leave London and get back to my hometown. I wanted to be near my son and family as I entered my thirties. It was the best thing I had ever done as even more amazing things started happening; both spiritually and work related.

I have recently gone on to work with two great London producers who are putting together some great tracks; writing lyrics and providing vocals for their tunes is proving to be an amazing and liberating journey. I've also had interest from one of the world's largest dance record labels and I've been given the opportunity to promote my music throughout Asia and Bollywood through one of the biggest Bollywood management teams. Just when I thought things couldn't get any better, I was asked, out of the blue, to host and produce a TV show on a subject that really interests me.

WOW! I'm finally getting my lucky breaks; through hard work, not just luck. I guess the luck comes from the energy you give out! It's all happening ten years later than I planned, but I learned a lot in those ten years; mostly about perseverance. There were plenty of times throughout my teens and early twenties when I wished that the world would end; there were days when I couldn't get out of bed (yes sometimes I still get those days), let alone have money to eat and life just seemed one big mess. But, you know; that's the beauty of life, the challenges and the days you find life a struggle are the moments that you find yourself imagining the life you desire; it was at those times that I truly felt most creative.

I have certainly come out of all these experiences a stronger, more fulfilled person, but I have to say, life isn't about making it a struggle and being rebellious; it's about having gratitude for wherever you may be, for family and friends that love and believe in you and about making your dreams come true.

It would be nice if we could make our dreams come true without all the hard work and dues that you have to pay. But the hard work is important, believe me! As long as you continue to put out the energy to achieve your dream role or job, then you will notice that the universe takes care and sees that and will give back to you amazing opportunities toward your goal. They are happening to me constantly.

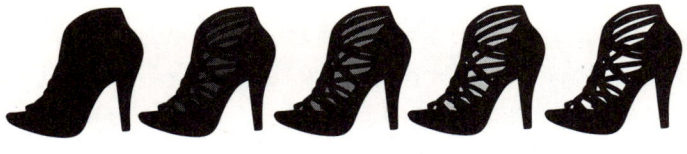

Elizabeth Grant

What made me start *Elizabeth Grant International*? I was a make-up artist and was happy in my job, when a bomb fell in the street alongside where I was walking during the Second World War. The left side of my face was badly injured. The doctors told me that my hearing was destroyed and that he would do his best; but I would be scarred. I was terribly miserable and upset; but not due to vanity. I was a make-up artist and I couldn't imagine that anyone would want me doing their make-up while I was so badly disfigured myself.

I was in my doctor's waiting room one day, looking at a medical journal and I read an article about a natural substance that had found some success treating war wounds. I wrote down the necessary information and took it to my then boyfriend; an analytical chemist.

At first, he wouldn't make it for me, stating that it wasn't for cosmetic purposes. After much begging and pleading, he relented and developed "Torricelumn®." The difference this product made was amazing; within eight months, it had actually repaired my skin.

Off I went, back to work and one day, I was talking to a film star as I was doing her make-up. We talked about the halogen lights used on film sets and what make-up does to the skin and she said, "You have a lovely skin."

I told her my story and she expressed interest in trying my "Torricelumn®", so I gave her some of mine. Two weeks later, the film star was raving about it, saying she had never used any product that was so wonderful. She immediately wanted to know where she could buy more.

It was at that moment that I realized I had something outstanding to share with the world. The rest, as the saying goes, is history. There have been many upsets along the way; life isn't smooth running. But as any boxer will tell you, if you fall, you get up, dust yourself off and start all over again. I absolutely refused to give up; not then and not now. I discovered that when you want to start a business, any business, you have to accept the fact that each day brings new challenges. It could be supplies arriving late, staff tantrums or any number of challenging setbacks. Anything can happen; too many things to talk about. You need to roll with the punches, so to speak; I do.

Not everyone is cut out to be 'Boss Material.' I am. I am kind, but firm. If there's a problem, I will work on it all night, if necessary. As I've said before, there is no manual for success; if there were, all you'd have to do is buy the book. Instead, you need old-fashioned guts, determination, willingness and the ability to talk to people. I have found that when problematic situations arise, sitting down with whoever has created the problem, eyeball to eyeball, you can straighten things out about 99% of the time.

Loving what I do gives me the power to carry on. As for my age, I simply ignore it. I'm not a fool, so I know that my top priority is good health; as long as my mind and body don't betray me, it's work as usual. I'm always being asked, "Why at your age (I am in my eighties as I write this) are you still working?" The answer is simple: I love what I'm doing.

What exactly am I doing? I'm out there spreading the word; I want every woman to believe me when I say that life is exciting and wonderful when you are in your 60's, 70's or 80's. I happen to be a very determined person who truly believes that women are wonderful creatures who have been given a raw deal. Why should we be subservient to men? What has always spurned me on is the fact that I know what I am capable of doing. Strangely enough, I am becoming more like my mother everyday. She was a very strong woman and she trained me well. There where no rules for her; she made her own rules…and so do I.

As a young girl, my mother would tell me never to settle for second best. She would say, "If you buy rubbish, you're left with rubbish.

Buy the best quality; even if it's old—it's still the best quality." With *Elizabeth Grant International*, it has to be the best; I will never settle for less. *EG* is successful because of the very principle: *Only The Best*. Always. I have never in 60 years of *Elizabeth Grant* put an advert in the paper. I have had lots of write-ups and testimonials from clients and beauty editors; but not once from me.

In my opinion, to be successful in business, you need insight, you have to be able to set, and meet, target goals and you need to be firm and kind with staff members. Life is a learning process and I am still learning; that's what makes it all so exciting. As a child, we had nothing; but I realize that when you're a child, you don't know that you're poor. You accept stale bread, hand-me-down clothing and you learn. I believe the person I am today is because having nothing as a child made me appreciate the value of everything today. When I was a young woman, I used to save, sometimes for up to a year to get what I wanted; always remembering my mother's words. When I started *EG*, I didn't look left or right; I looked straight ahead. I was very determined; knowing that my product was wonderful and that I had something to share with the world.

So when a man said to me, "Have you got a million dollars? Because that's what you'll need to start a skin care line." I replied, "I don't have a million dollars, but what I do have is Torricelumn®; something so wonderful that I won't let anything or anyone stop me from being successful!"

I believe in myself and I also believe that luck has played a part in my life too. My childhood was poor and I left school when I was 13-years-old and from that day on, I had to work; but even with all of that, I consider myself a very lucky person. I try to make each day a happy day. Mind you, this doesn't always happen; nevertheless, I do laugh a lot. Nobody likes a misery and, of course, loving what you do is *vital*.

How many times have you heard, "Thank God it's Friday," and, "oh Hell, tomorrow is Monday?" If that's how you feel, you will never have a successful business. I can't wait to get to the office in the morning; it's always been like that. I suppose you can call it enthusiasm. Even today when we bring out something new, I am always looking, seeking to find the best and most innovative ideas—I still get excited. To me, age, be it, 20 or 80, is only a number—and for me I choose to ignore it.

There is, of course, no manual for success; so write your own manual. A sense of humor is essential. I'm not going to pretend that my life is one big bed of roses. I have my own way of dealing with stress or something nasty that has happened. What I do is write it all down. For instance, if I wanted to tell someone exactly what I thought of them, I might write down everything I wanted to say and I address it to that person, but I never post it. I do, however, always read the letter the next day; strangely enough, it always seems so …distant. The issue turns out to be not *that* awful anymore, not *that* terrible—it turns out, not something I couldn't handle. With that, like clockwork, I rip up the letter, tear it to shreds and just feel so much better.

I find life can be beautiful; I enjoy my life and I *love EG*! So, I will carry on. Retirement, to me, is a dirty word. I will never retire. Life is too exciting. *Elizabeth Grant* is exciting. Making women look wonderful is what I consider to be my life's work.

The strange thing about being successful is that at no time did I think about the money side of it all. All I thought about was the fact that I have something wonderful, that somehow I must find a way to share this with everyone. There is a saying, "Fool's rush in where angels fear to tread." If that is true, then I am a fool; because it never occurred to me that money is needed to start anything. But when you are determined; when you are capable and focused, as I was, and still am—somehow, somewhere, you do manage to get started. In my case, it was sheer determination and guts. I may be in my 80's but my business and lab are the latest things in Science and Technology. I am always interested in, "What's new, Doc?" But that's just me and my attitude towards life.

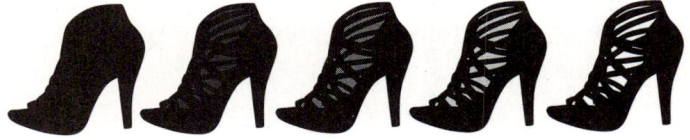

Stella Telleria

Over the years, many people have asked me how I landed the dream job I have. I'm an Artistic Director for the largest hair care service company in the world and the only Artistic Director for my branch of the company within Canada. I'd coveted this position for years and was fortunate to have secured the position by the time I was 23. In my experience, the path to success is a long, thankless journey that many lose patience with before they ever reach the payoff. I know it sounds like I achieved success at quite a young age, but it was still a long journey.

I set out on my path unknowingly in my sophomore year of high school. I had decided to take Cosmetology since I still had some room on my schedule. I suppose the reason I made that choice was so that I could finally figure out how to tame my unruly, 'Chia Pet' hair. Domesticating my wild, curly hair seemed like a good plan at the time.

I discovered a talent for hairstyling; while others struggled with the basics, I breezed through the lessons effortlessly. Soon, my classmates were asking me to show them how to do four stranded braids and perm sectioning. I was teaching others how to do things I had just learnt to do myself. Throughout high school, I would be called in at lunch hours to work on clients. I would perm and style hair for students at grad time and for class pictures. I competed twice in the Skills Canada competitions, but I never thought I would ever pursue a job in the hair industry. I wasn't sure what I wanted to do with my future yet.

Graduation came and went and I had been rejected from the program I wanted to take in college. I didn't know what I was going to do, but I knew I didn't want to keep working at the fast food restaurant

I had worked at through high school. I started applying for different jobs to tide me over until I figured out what I was going to take the following year in college. None of the jobs caught my eye or stood out in any special way.

One day, my mother mentioned in passing that I should apply at a hair salon. I didn't think anyone would hire me, so I handed out some resumes and didn't stress about the expectation of a reply. The first salon to call me back was the one I currently work for. I went in for an interview and everyone seemed very nice. I got the job. The manager gave me a bunch of haircutting videos to watch and study. I looked at the stack of videos.

"So what exactly will I be doing on Monday when I start? Will I be answering the phones, sweeping and shampooing hair?"

I knew I was probably going to start as a receptionist or an assistant for a while, so that I could observe things and learn from the other stylists. My Cosmetology instructor had told us that this was how most apprentices start off in the industry.

"Oh, no; you're going to be on the floor, cutting and styling hair." The manager smiled at me and I could have sworn I was close to losing my lunch.

I cleared my suddenly dry throat. "Um, you realize that I've done very little haircutting, right? I mostly did perms and long hair styling in Cosmo class." I was sure that she had simply misunderstood my experience level. My stomach settled as I reassured myself and my nerves calmed down a bit.

"No worries, you'll learn how to cut hair, that's what the videos are for." Dread filled every nerve in my body until it felt like every muscle would begin twitching.

I took the videos home and watched them as if my life depended on it. There were seven videos in total. I watched them all before Monday and as the weekend drew to a close, my trepidation was a physical presence.

Monday came and I showed up at my new job on time, with some scissors that had come from a drugstore-bought clipper set. I had no clue what I was walking into. I can look back and laugh now, but at the time, I was sweating bullets and just hoping to do the best job I could.

I remember my first client. I was so nervous, I was shaking like I was about to face a firing squad. I began combing her hair and suddenly I couldn't remember a thing I'd watched on any of the videos I'd taken home. I somehow managed to get through the haircut without any serious events. I'm sure I looked petrified to that poor client; she probably felt bad for me. The girl I was working with noticed the scissors I was using and quickly lent me a pair of her own to use until I could buy my own professional shears.

The first haircut had gone by in a blur of nerves. What I remember with crystal clarity was my second client that day. As she sat down at my station, I fumbled with the cape in my hands. I dropped the cape and quickly picked it up off the floor. She looked at me like I was from another planet. I tried to stay calm. I draped her with the cape and asked her how she would like her haircut. She wanted to keep the same style she currently had; she just needed a little trim. I laid out a plan of action in my mind; I would just follow the lines of her previous haircut and remove the little amount of hair she wanted.

I began dampening her hair and she stared at me as if she were deciding how to use her laser vision to burn me into cinders. I became even more nervous and must have been shaking; I took a few snips at the hair at the nape of her neck, when her head turned to me.

"How long have you been doing this?" Her voice was accusing, her eyebrow scrunched, her mouth purred into a pout. I imagined I was wide-eyed and pale as death.

I swallowed hard. "I've been doing hair for about a year." My voice was a squeak. My answer was honest; the three semesters I had done in high school amounted to about a year.

Her eyes narrowed and she turned her face back to the mirror and glared at my reflection in it. "I can tell by the way you're holding that comb you don't know *what* you're doing." Her voice was like venom. I had gone numb.

She began running her hands through her hair, inspecting what little I had cut. "Is there still hair back there?" Her voice had taken on an even harsher edge.

I struggled to find my voice. "I only cut the very ends; like you asked." I tried to show her the bits of her hair that still clung to my wet fingers so she could see how little I had taken off. But it was like the air had the consistency of molasses; I moved slowly, frozen in horror.

"Is there someone else here who knows how to cut hair and can finish *this*?" She sighed and breathed deeply like a bull waiting to charge. Anger rose like steam around her head.

I could no longer locate my voice. I nodded at her and ran to the back room where the other stylist was sitting, reading a magazine. She looked startled as she glanced up at me.

"Um, can you finish that lady's haircut?" My voice broke.

Instantly the she understood the situation. "Sure. Just sit down, okay?" She stared at me with kind, wide eyes.

Again, I just nodded.

She took care of the client and I closed the door to the back room as she left. I just wanted to hide. I sank down into a chair and cried. Why was I even here? I couldn't cut hair. I felt so humiliated. I'd never be able to do this. I blocked out the noise coming from the front of the shop. I couldn't bear to listen to what was being said about me. I was utterly devastated. I had been wounded so personally; I felt like a complete idiot.

That might have seemed like an overreaction to some; as if I was just being an emotional, little girl. No hairstylist wakes up in the morning and says to themselves, "I'm going to ruin someone's hair today!" We so desperately want to please our clients that when this doesn't happen we take it personally; it can be difficult not to let it affect us. I had always excelled in Cosmo class; I'd always had top marks and had even been offered a scholarship. It was earth shattering to hear how terrible I was at something I had thought I was so good at. It made me question my abilities and worth.

The eventual chime of the front door signaled that the client had gone, but I made no move to open the back door. The other stylist came into the back room and sat on a nearby chair. I couldn't look at her. I had tears running down my face.

"So what happened?" She asked softly.

I explained the whole situation to her and she listened without interrupting.

"You didn't do anything wrong, the client just panicked." She gave me a sad smile. "We've all been where you are. People can be mean. When that happens, you come to the back room and cry your eyes out for a bit. Then, when you're ready, you go back out there and do another haircut. Okay?"

I paused. "Okay."

Now, when I reflect, I realize that I never thought of quitting. The thought had never entered my mind and when I look back, I think that was quite odd. Quitting was a natural response when coming up against something like that.

Once I had calmed down and had salvaged what little was left of my self-esteem, I went back out to cut another client's hair. This time, when the woman sat down in my chair and could see my trembling hands, she smiled at me.

"Are you new?" She asked.

I didn't bother telling her how long I'd been doing hair. "Yeah, I'm new here." I gave her the opportunity to ask for someone else before I'd even touched her hair.

She didn't ask for the other stylist; instead, as I cut her hair, she told me what a good job I was doing. She smiled and seemed generally delighted with her haircut. She even asked me for my card, so she could come back to me. I don't know if that woman ever really understood what her kindness meant to me on that day, but it gave me the courage to keep moving forward.

I had kept my other job at the fast food place; in case hairdressing didn't work out. I was having regular dreams and nightmares about cutting hair. I dreamt that I was at the restaurant and hair started shooting out of the fryers and bunches of hair were rolled up as the patties in the burgers. I'd wake up in the middle of the night, under the impression that I had to get to the salon and cut hair. I had even caught myself mimicking the motions of cutting hair in my sleep.

Eventually, my confidence grew and the dreams stopped. I took every opportunity available with the company. I signed up for an advanced haircutting class offered by the salon chain. That was when I discovered exactly where I wanted to go within the company. The instructor of the class was professional and kind. She taught me so much and encouraged me to excel. She was an Artistic Director and at that moment, I knew that was what I wanted to be. Such a position was not easy to come by; the instructor had been the Artistic Director for years and hers was the only such position in Canada.

I continued working in the salon while I attended school, wrote all my exams and became a licensed hairstylist. I competed for my company in haircutting competitions and displayed the trophies I brought back at my workstation. I strove to improve my skills; taking each haircut I did and evaluating what I had done that had worked well and what I would do differently next time. I always saw room for improvement. I didn't let fear stop me from taking any client. Haircuts and services stylists would avoid I would accept. I was never afraid of failing, I had realized that that was the only way I could improve my skills. If I avoided things like so many of the other stylists, I would be avoiding them forever. Fear is a byproduct of inexperience; you're only scared because you haven't done it enough.

Years passed and I began to tire of my position. I enjoyed my job, but I felt that I had already learnt all that I could from it. I still harboured a secret desire to be an Artistic Director, whose job it was to travel all over the country, teaching and inspiring other stylists. But my chances at such a job were slim. There were stylists from twenty-four salons to choose from, not to mention that the current Artistic Director was going nowhere.

I eventually went back to college and took Marketing. I had graduated and was determined to change careers; but something held me back. Soon, I heard of a woman that had worked with the company for years who had recently quit. She had been a Certified Technical Trainer; the position directly under the Artistic Director. I was talking about the open position with another stylist when she told me that I should apply for it. Why the idea had never occurred to me, I'll never know; possibly due to the fact that I was getting ready to move on with my life. I called up the Area Supervisors and explained my interest in the position that had just become available. They were thrilled to hear that I was interested in the job and were pleased that I had shown such initiative. I never realized that simply asking about the position was considered initiative. I had beaten many other more senior stylists to the position simply because I had been the first one to ask about it. Seniority had made some of the stylists expect to simply receive the position once it was available. Yet another lesson learnt; an ego can be a very detrimental thing.

I interviewed with both Area Supervisors and was offered the position. Along with the job, they wanted me to manage one of the salons; as it would show a serious commitment to the company.

Management was never something I was interested in. I realized that if I ever wanted to be an Artistic Director I would have to do some things I didn't want to do to show that I was dependable and responsible enough for the job. Managing the salon meant some very late nights and always being available for staff and salon issues. Management is a thankless job where one tends to be the scapegoat for anything that could possibly go wrong. I cannot begin to describe all the challenges that I dealt with as a manager. There were many times that I thought all my long hours and efforts were going unnoticed.

I became a Manager and a CTT at the same time. I was flown to the U.S. for training and my connecting flight was cancelled because of tornado warnings. I was stranded in the wrong city in terrible weather with no luggage and to top it off, I was going to miss part of the training class I had come for. The next day, I got to my destination in the suit I had been wearing for two days; with disheveled hair, no make up and teetering uncomfortably in a pair of brand new, high heeled shoes. What an impression I must have made. I thought I might actually die of acute foot agony; since that moment, I travel comfortably dressed.

I had missed half of the first day and had to stay late to catch up on the information I'd missed and I was going on three hours of sleep.

I pulled through and ended up making a fabulous impression on the Artistic Director who was training me. Another lesson learnt; nobody wants to hear you complain. Never, ever complain. Keep your cool and others will notice.

I returned home and worked hard at the two new positions I now had. I managed a busy salon and one week out of every month, I would teach a haircutting class. CTT's taught classes part time, whereas the Artistic Director trained others on a full time basis. The current Artistic Director was on maternity leave and I was helping out with covering some of the classes she taught.

The first class I taught was a group of five stylists, most of who were older than me and a few who had been in the industry longer than I had been. Again, I could feel my nerves fray a bit. What if I messed up? What if I couldn't control the class? What if they didn't take me seriously? I concentrated on thinking positive. When someone asked me a question I didn't have the answer for, I was honest and told her I didn't know. I was worried that she would think I wasn't qualified or knowledgeable enough to instruct the class. She told me that she liked that I admitted to not knowing the answer to her question; she liked that I wasn't pretending to be a know-it-all. Sometimes we think we need all the answers; but what we really need is an open mind to listen to the answers and input of others.

My first class of students all pitched in and bought me a present. It was a cake pedestal and I still have it to this day; five years later.

I still wanted to be an Artistic Director and when it was time for the current Artistic Director to come back from maternity leave, I was disappointed. I really did like her, so I was happy she would be returning, but it meant that I wouldn't be teaching as many classes, since she would be reclaiming hers.

It turned out that during her maternity leave she had gotten pregnant again and had decided not to return to work.

I interviewed over the phone with the company's Senior Artistic Director for the position. She was like a celebrity within our company. It had been her I'd watched years ago in all those haircutting tapes before my very first shift as a hairstylist. I was so nervous; but I nailed the interview and after some patient waiting, I finally got the job I'd always wanted. I was so elated you couldn't beat the smile off my face. I traveled for three full months to train for the position and to this day I enjoy it still.

I've found that what worked for me was to remember that success is hidden in the everyday mundane things one does at work. It was about doing my job and remembering to do the right thing as often as I could; even when I didn't feel like it. It was about not developing an ego; which is career suicide, in my opinion. If you have to work too hard to convince others how good you are; chances are you're not all that good. Never take yourself too seriously; everyone messes up, it's practically the law. Never be afraid to make mistakes. I can tell someone why something isn't a good idea a hundred different ways, but until that person actually experiences it for themselves, they will never truly understand. If something scares you, you must tackle that something until it no longer does. Fear comes from inexperience and neither will get you anywhere. Always look for room and opportunities to improve no matter how small they might be; it will make a difference. Jump at every opportunity to get involved; the reward may not be visible at the moment but it will be someday. Most importantly, don't give up. You never know how close you may have been to your goal, one more push or stride might have landed you in the winner's circle and you never would have known if you just gave up.

Tanya Marwah

How does one succeed in a family full of successful entrepreneurs? One grandfather owned leather factories in India, the other owned a construction company. I have an uncle with a large tool and die factory, while another uncle is a prominent and well-respected accountant. Each of their children, all sons, joined their respective family businesses and prospered.

It was naturally taken for granted that sons would join in the family business; but when a South Asian girl wanted to do the same, a lot of questions were asked. I wasn't taken seriously and everyone assumed that it was a short term occupation. As a result, I had to work twice as hard to prove that I was serious.

Why would I give up on my passion? I love what I do! My life is my work and as a result, I wake up each day brimming with new ideas and solutions to the previous days' problems. I am infused with energy and enthusiasm. Today, at this stage in my life, I am very happy to be where I am.

The success I enjoy now is built on the foundation of my lonely teen years. I'm an only child and spent much of my time alone. My parents helped me through the tough times; becoming my best friends, confidantes and mentors. I was extremely conscious of my looks and had an inferiority complex; I found social situations extremely difficult. I used to fantasize about being a successful entrepreneur whose looks weren't important. I created several scrapbooks filled with people that I met or admired and jotted down what I liked about them; whether it was their business tactics or their demeanor. I was turning myself into a more insightful businesswoman.

I felt that I was living two lives; at *Marla's*, our clothing boutique, I was this fabulous fashion diva who knew everything about the latest trends and styles in the fashion world. The stylists who worked in the store did my makeup and hair and told me what products to use to help me with my complexion and acne. They were my second family; the sisters I had never had and always looked up to. Once I arrived home and washed off my glamorous mask and the real me surfaced. I always tried to mimic what I learned from my pseudo life, but I could never look the same and I was always laughed at in school. I wanted out of that life and into the real world *fast*! I wanted a fresh start; I decided to re-invent myself and start the next chapters in my life living up to the image I wanted to portray: Strong, successful, and glamourous!

University provided me with the necessary business skills and helped increase my confidence and maturity. I met a lot of influential professors that honed in on my entrepreneurial spirit. I read every business book and journal that they recommended. I was like a sponge, soaking in as much business knowledge as possible from them. I started to understand the techniques other successful business entrepreneurs used and how to improve on them; whether by using business philosophies from *Wal-Mart's* founder, Sam Walton, to understanding Margaret Whitman's masterminding of *E-Bay*, or mimicking Donald Trump's aggressive approach to business. I was laying the groundwork for my future endeavours.

One might think that I was lucky to be born into a successful business, but I had to work very hard for my position! I have worked in the company from a young age and started from the ground up. That was the best hands-on experience that I could have received. I learned about customer analysis, negotiating, selling, leadership, motivation, market analysis and customer service.

From a young age, I learned how to respect the stylists that work in the stores, the fashion and what our company's objectives were. I didn't take anything for granted. My family realized that I understood what hard work was and passed on the Retail division to me. This was a major milestone and the beginning of a new chapter in my life. I had been working and preparing for it all my life.

Taking care of the Retail Sector was a completely different ball game. A lot was entailed because every decision I made had an effect on the performance of the store. The challenge was to prove that I had the management skills to run the division. I had to be up-to-date with the trends and make sure that the operation ran smoothly.

I wanted to change the objectives of our company and concentrate more on e-commerce and customer service. Convincing my parents that it was a good idea was one of the biggest hurdles I had to overcome. How does one change the mindset of two people who have been in the business for over 25 years? Their attitude was more of an old school approach and they were content with the level of success that they had already attained. I had higher ideals! I felt that there was so much more potential with e-commerce flourishing and branding becoming more of an integral role and I wanted to take retailing international, rather than local. I wanted to expand our mid-size corporation into a fashion empire. I envisioned a one-stop shop for a glamorous diva out for the night. Instead of just selling a dress to someone, I wanted to sell an experience to this individual. She would have her own stylist who knew her name, size and tastes. At the end of her fashion experience with us, she would have the 'it' dress with the right shoes, accessories and makeup. This concept would give *Marla's* that competitive advantage. But, imagine trying to sell the idea to two individuals who have created such a success from nothing.

The initial talks didn't start out well. I wanted to increase expenses by having more stylists on the sales floor to create that personal shopping experience for our customer. Working at the store level, I believed that if the customers were happy, we would profit. They wanted to have more emphasis on clothing and merchandising. After much tug and pull, they decided to test it out in one store.

It didn't work, initially and I was just stunned. What had happened? Where had I gone wrong? I couldn't believe that my first corporate decision had been such a failure! After a couple of weeks, I realized my mistake. I knew that there were two things that make a company successful; customers and the team that works for you. Understanding and respecting one's customers is paramount. But most importantly, the stylists are the front line forces that help create the image of the store.

Instead of telling the stylists what to do, I asked them how they would create a more personable and fun experience. After a couple of weeks, it started to work out and there was an improvement because they were having more fun and working harder since they had come up with all the ideas.

As an entrepreneur, it is gratifying to have a good team, able to brainstorm and contribute different ideas toward creating a healthy and extremely competitive company. "Have Fun" is a mantra that I repeat several times a day. I say it to the stylists if they are helping a customer and I say it to our clothing designers when we're choosing designs for the upcoming seasons. We've all gone through tough times, whether coming from broken homes, facing bullying, racism or abuse. Those are some of the life experiences that mold us into being what we become. Don't look to the past; but use it as a stepping stone to soar to the sky and achieve all your dreams and fantasies. Remember to have fun!

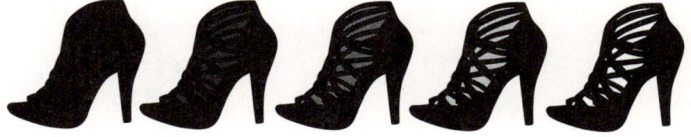

Lisa Bradburn

The following has been written as a conversation between Lisa and her alter ego.

Dear Lisa

We have been together since the dawn of our existence and I know every intimate detail about you. It is at this point in time that I am compelled to write and thank you for the lessons you've taught me during the vast influx of joy, despair and all other emotions that have made up our lives together.

Not long ago, physical and physiological changes began to surface within me; much as the spring thaw cracks ice on a frozen lake. It started when the light caught my reflection in the mirror to reveal frail lines around the eyes. Silver strands sprang from the undergrowth of my hair and you shamelessly plucked them out. The aging process is creeping in. Neither of us is immune. After cupping my face with your warm, gentle hands, you had seen enough to know. Your words cut through me as a knife slices butter, 'Stop wasting time.'

Was I ever doing this? Yes, I must have been. You told me a story that remains cemented in my mind; it was about your banking career. The suit may have looked good on you, but the job didn't. One day, you pushed back your chair, walked solemnly into your Manager's office and shut the door with purpose. You said,

"Look, it's nothing personal; you're a great leader, but I'm no longer inspired and I have no passion. I quit."

Then you left. People thought you had two screws loose, but it didn't hold you back. That day, I saw the truth in your eyes and knew you were right. Every time I pass that dominating tower reaching for the skyline, I smile; for you.

After some time had passed, I had the chance occasion to see you through a shop window. There you were, strutting along with a tune in your head. I didn't see an iPod. When I asked what brought you happiness, you quietly replied, 'Every path is different.' My immediate thought was negative. Sure; everyone knows that, big deal.

As the day progressed, I noticed growing resentment. It was the realization that I was alone in the world. My friends were falling in love and marrying; children were being born. Was I missing out on the essentials of life? At night, I laid in the darkness with my eyes closed, attempting to shut out reality; but all I could see were your words skating around in my mind. I hated you. For days, Lisa, your statement wouldn't depart amidst my own self-loathing. I noticed that as I focused on these inner woes, other life ambitions wouldn't progress. So I halted, dead in my tracks and began to believe. It was only then that life changed for the better. This time, I shed a passing tear; for you.

One evening, we went to a charity gala together. You paid so much attention to detail; your hair, your dress, your makeup. It felt contrived. For a woman who appears to possess so much wisdom, I admit, you left me confused. Across the room, I watched you chase the unobtainable and shook my head in disbelief that you had fallen for these falsehoods. When I confronted you on your behavior, you became an oxymoron,

'Be authentic.'

How could you have let me down? The one person I admire and trust. The next day, your eyes were glazed over, foggy as you sat next to me, drinking coffee and cursing. I was the one holding up the pieces. For a second time, I sought the truth. Through clenched teeth you revealed a lust for power, seeking out companions who possess such worldly charms, always leading to your demise. I applauded your honesty; even your authenticity. From that moment on, there was a difference. You laid aside these childish notions and became strong again. A glass was raised; to you.

Sometimes Lisa, you make me laugh. I called you on the phone, but you couldn't hear me. Instead you shouted, meet me at the corner! So we met, face to face. Upon our greeting, you mentioned an accident whereby a piece of cotton had become wedged in your ear causing partial hearing impairment. This small misfortune had become your fascination. You claimed it had altered your perception of the world as it forced you to pay greater attention to the people around you. Even now you cling to the spoken word, expressed emotion or action. When I asked, what could this all mean, you winked, 'Listen and learn.'

I set forth to prove your observation wrong and for a day, taped my ears shut. Granted, my balance was off and I tumbled around the subway like a drunkard. When a man pushed me aside and mouthed the words, 'Excuse me,' I began to face up to my short-term disability. Yes; attention to others is a requirement of life. It helps to prove our own existence. Now, I watch the mouths of those speaking, drinking in their syllables. I strive to listen, digest and allow fellow mankind to feel special by the presence of the moment. I learned something new and took a bow; for you.

I know, I know; you get tired of my whining. When I want something so bad, but feel it is beyond my reach, you take my hand and cock your head; like you don't understand. You went away for a weekend film-writing course and returned energized, focused and ready for action. Your determination made me feel weak; spending every evening tucked away in your tiny apartment stroking the keys. I wanted my ego stroked. You noticed my frown and threw back your hair, chuckling at my insecurities,

'Become an expert in one field, spend 10,000 hours.'

What; now you're the Riddler? No, you said this comment was for my own good. To realize that aspirations are worth fighting for, talent requires effort and time to germinate. Again, I mocked you and questioned whether you prefer your own company to the rest of humanity; it certainly seemed so. I liked that you refused my query and promptly retorted that mediocrity is too prevalent in this world and you expect excellence of yourself, your work. As we spoke, the rain fell heavy around us and I tipped my hat; toward you.

You've distanced yourself away from particular individuals. A few old comrades have fallen to the wayside. When summoned, you chirped that time is a rare commodity; valued more than oil or gold. Frugal bitch, is this why I was ignored? No longer worthy of your presence? These new patterns of behavior, aligning yourself with those who appear to have relevance on the social stage disturb me. Yes, I'm purposely being harsh toward you in an attempt to probe further; are you behind their actions or protecting your reputation? You claim there are two parts; to always question the deep motives that you acknowledge as necessary certainties and purposely seek out those that adhere to these principals. I deciphered your message as one who should,

'Be careful of the company you keep.'

I took stock of all personal acquaintances, family and past lovers and recalled your ramblings on the follies of time wasting. The guilt. Oh Lisa, how could I have been so blind? Those brief moments, weeks, months and years dissolving into nothing; blank space. I could be so much further ahead than I am now. Recognizing my frustration, you tousled my hair and made me realize I am still in the prime of my youth. How wonderful to possess this self-awareness today, than suffer the sorrow of acknowledgement decades later. We sat in silence at the edge of an ancient lake. I picked up a perfect, small flat stone to skip and made a wish; for you.

Do you remember the time I walked in on you? I'm sorry; I caught you slumped over in bed, speaking to yourself and I wondered if you were losing your marbles. No, you weren't. You were in conversation with the air and didn't want to be disturbed. Shouldn't you be in church; the venue to speak to the Divine One? I was determined to find out if you were getting a response from the other end. To this you replied, "Of course; all in due time." Patience is not built into human DNA, but we must have hope of what will come. This faith placed in the hands of the great unknown frightened me. You asked, "Have we really changed in a thousand years? Do we not encompass the same emotions as the Romans?" You lunged forward, 'Faith is relevant in modern times.'

I cannot subscribe to your thoughts. The prophets of today look no further than our inner core for essential truths. The media perpetuates the ideal to focus on thy self. How is the world so wrong and you're so right? You took a step back; a deep breath. Sigh; pace yourself and let's start again. You posed a simple test. Take one small challenge and seek the guidance of this spirit, to whichever name and gender you want to assign. Focus on this task and continually request assistance, knowing that an outcome will transpire. What you want may not necessarily be what you get, but a reply will come forth all the same. I accepted your challenge with an open mind, recalling a recent hurtful argument with my mother. Throughout that week, I considered my issue from all angles with this silent partner. It became present, listening. To my shock, I confessed the areas where I had faltered. Before the week was over, a grand reconciliation was made. We forgave each other and moved on. Maybe there is something to this. Maybe I was making it far too complicated. I found a new friend in the force and will remain true; because of you.

For a while, you were worried. I didn't show up, a card wasn't sent and an email was unreturned when I promised I would. You blamed my absence on this technologically advanced era of 'maybe.' Perhaps we're subscribing to a new system that makes avoidance easy. When did it become so difficult to say Yes or No? Or to commit to a firm decision? You cornered me one day to get a rise, but all I gave you was disappointment after uttering two short words, 'I'm busy.' Bullshit; you're only as busy as you want to be. This word should be permanently erased from the English language as it perpetuates a false sense of importance. The topic hit a nerve and you weren't about to give up when I heard you say,

'Follow through on your word.'

Guilty as charged; you'd got me. I confessed despite my back being up against the wall. In typical fashion, you remained calm, stoic against my stubbornness. You quipped, "The first step to recovery is admitting your weaknesses." I didn't want to tell you this, but you sounded like a walking AA meeting. All I did was forget to send a lousy card. It doesn't matter; it's the principal. That day you taught me to keep my word golden. I'll never promise anything I can't deliver, no matter how grade two; for you.

You and I were sitting on a park bench sharing a lovely spring afternoon while discreetly scoping out the fit men in tight jogging shorts; for research purposes. We were using *The Economist* as a shield, should one stop and assume some level of intelligence. As I peered beyond the pages of *Lexicon,* one particular factual statement jumped off the page, which claimed that over 90% of the world's CEO's are male. I recall you tipping the bench in laughter given the shock on my face. You teased me and stole the Blahnik off my foot, waving it in the air like a screeching idiot, 'High heels can crush glass ceilings.'

Settle down; you're embarrassing. I didn't ask for your two cents, but you gave it anyway. It started with, 'when I was younger.' What are you, a dinosaur? You're only 33. You claimed that in your twenties you wanted to rule the roost; hold the corporate keys to the castle. Now, you say? Nah; let the A type boys and girls dominate. The stress of ambition will eventually catch up to their hearts. Why did you lose your spark? Oh, you foolish one. I will never lose my edge, but I have seen the greater perspective. It begins with this long, unscathed lifeline etched deep within my palm. We paused; I asked you if I was missing the point. No, you leaned forward in your seat. Look, at the end of your life, do you want to be known as the woman who shrewdly maneuvered through the conglomerate ranks or the lady with a dynamic personality that made people laugh so hard their belly ached? Can't you be both? Of course; but I'd rather focus my attention on the latter. Your preference was clear. The Queen of the Corporates had died. Even today, your pursuit is to entertain, teach and provoke humanity through your craft. I respect your decision and we have settled our discourse. Now I know what to do; through you.

My dear old friend, it is time to close off. How far we have come and yet, I have faith the majority of our journey still lies ahead. I anticipate a multitude of profound and gut wrenching moments. You know; the ones that cause laugh lines to be etched deep within the forehead.

Here's to many more lessons, Lisa.
Sincerely,
Your neurotic self.

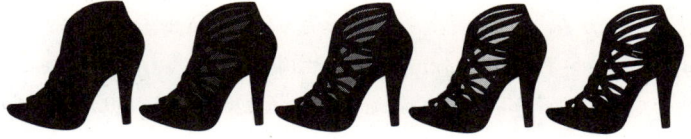

Julie Christine

Everyone grows up differently. We all come from different kinds of families, have different experiences and we all develop different views of the world around us as a result of our environment.

Some people seem to have all the luck and others seem to struggle from the moment they take their first breath. I would place myself somewhere in the middle of the scale. My childhood wasn't an easy one. I wouldn't say my life has been extremely easy either.

I was a troubled kid; scared and anxious for much of the time. As a teenager, I was angry with the world. I did poorly in school; not because I wasn't smart, but because I didn't care. Maybe it would have been more accurate to say that I felt I wasn't cared for. I was defiant and rude and I liked to cause trouble. I liked to push the limits to see how much I could get away with. Negative attention was still attention of some kind.

I remember being determined that when I became an adult, I would listen to kids the way I wanted to be listened to as a teen. I would do everything differently than my parents had done. I would be different than my teachers and guidance counselors and I would change the world one kid at a time, because I knew how it felt to be a kid. I knew what it was like to be misunderstood. What I didn't realize was that I was missing a few pieces to the puzzle. At 34, I'm still missing some pieces to the puzzle. I wonder how many times people say to themselves, "If I'd known then what I know now…"

Thankfully, along the way I learned some pretty amazing values that have brought me to where I am today. I may be a few pieces short of a puzzle; but still successful.

I was lucky to have had a few very significant people in my life who have allowed me the opportunity to adopt some of their virtues for myself. Qualities like kindness, gratitude, loyalty, tact and fortitude.

I had an amazing grandfather. He was a kind and gentle man. He always sang, *"You are my Sunshine"* to me as a little girl and that is how I believe he always felt about me. Although he could be gentle and kind, that didn't in any way forfeit his ability to tell it like it was whether you wanted to hear it or not. Grandpa had firm beliefs and wasn't afraid to share them; especially if he saw you making a wrong turn. Stringent and coarse advice was borne of deep love and worry. He was meticulous in all areas of his life. His home and belongings were always in order. His finances were carefully planned and he painstakingly carried out that plan without ever losing sight of his goals. He was a man of fortitude and forged ahead in the most tumultuous of times. He was loyal; his hard work was for his wife and family. Because he held such strong work ethics, he expected the same from others.

He was a man I learned a great deal from. He told me a story often that I believe had some influence on my career choices today. When he was very young and things were very different, he too was a troublemaker. Once he was picked up by the police for throwing rocks at a milk truck and taken into what was custody, back then. He was brought forward before the judge and was going to be sent away to our equivalent of adolescent detention, a boys' home, for quite a long time. The *Big Brothers Association* was very different back then; they stepped in and took responsibility for him. It was something that he never forgot. The *Big Brothers* became the charity that he donated to every year for the rest of his life. There help must have had quite an impact on him. He had quite an impact on me.

Somehow, I'm not sure how, I finished high school with a diploma. I didn't attend my prom because I had never really enjoyed high school; I figured, why bother?

I still had an idea that I was going to change the world; the world of children, anyway. I found a Child and Youth Worker program at a local college that seemed to fit my plan. I found that about 2500 people applied to the program and there were about 36 available spots. To get in, there were interviews, group interviews, an autobiography and, of course, high school marks. I was in bad shape for the high school marks. For the first time in my life, I felt a strong sense of determination to accomplish something that was positive. I worked my butt off on the essay and I kicked butt in the interviews. Although I only made it to a waiting list for that September, by January I was in and starting college.

College was a completely different experience for me. I was taking classes that I enjoyed on subjects that I had chosen, instead of someone picking them for me. I aced all three years, with never a lower mark than a B+. I had an enormous amount of fun along the way.

Part of my college program involved work placements and I spent those placements in a home for abused women; a closed custody jail for young offenders and a short term intake and assessment home for children just removed from their homes by the Children's Aid. I couldn't even begin to describe the things I witnessed and the stories I heard about during my times at these places.

During college, I was hired as relief at a group home for teenage boys. I was actually hired by my future husband; but I wouldn't know that until years later. I didn't like him when I met him; I tease him about that now. He has always been a spirited, hard working man who isn't afraid to speak his mind. The people who take the time to get to know him will discover the amazing love and loyalty he shows. Every client I ever knew who crossed his path developed a unique and amazingly special relationship with Steve.

The group home was out in the country on twelve acres of beautiful property and housed ten teenage boys, aged 12–18. These boys were what some referred to as the 'worst of the worst.' They were hard to serve adolescents with severe behavioural and psychiatric difficulties. Over the next seven years, I saw some of the scariest, saddest and strangest things I will probably ever experience in that group home.

Those boys could become extremely violent at times; requiring the staff to physically restrain them in order to prevent themselves or others from becoming hurt. They would hit, bite and spit on us and damage property at times.

It was quite something to try to explain to others that despite their behaviour at times, they could be the most likeable boys. Each one had unique qualities and talents. They all had emotions and feelings and they all missed their families. They were simply human beings that started out on the 'bad luck' end of the scale.

It was also during this time that I learned a lot about my level of patience and how to manage my stress levels. I decided after my first year of working at the home that some martial arts would serve me very well in that environment. I had never been exposed to church or religion growing up and when I stepped into the dojo with ponds and koi, waterfalls and rock gardens and a Sensei of such old fashioned eastern standards, I knew I had found my church.

I had come to learn self-defense and I did. But I took a lot more from that man than punching and kicking. Loyalty, respect and gratitude were the more important things I learned from the man I call my Sensei. I learned that each moment is the only moment; each moment is the last moment.

It wasn't about breaking boards or how many trophies one could win. When I stepped inside, the dojo became the battlefield. The mental training involved in the kata's we preformed and the hard physical training prepared us to fight life. That was where the battle really took place. I was taught that life is a struggle; but to persevere. To enjoy the good times that life brings and that to win is within. I developed balance and self discipline.

I trained in other arts, such as tai chi and yoga; these helped with balance and managing stress. I have studied the arts for about fifteen years and earned my second degree black belt, but I really feel as though I'm just a beginner and could train for another fifteen years and only scratch the surface. Regardless, this art and this man called Sensei gave me direction. They provided a foundation that I didn't have before. It was a place from which to start and virtues from which to live by. I think this is what all religions strive to do and have in common.

After college, I continued to work at the group home. I moved away from home and into an apartment by myself and I absolutely loved my independence. I got a dog that kept me company and that was all I needed. The kids at work kept me busy enough.

I had begun to date my husband, Steve, a few years before but independence was an experience I wasn't willing to give up too soon. I needed to know the struggle of making my own way, paying my own bills, making my own mistakes and learning my own lessons.

Independence lasted two years before I decided to move in with Steve. We lived together for three years.

Eventually, we married and had a beautiful girl of our own. Added to the two daughters Steve has from a previous marriage, we were an instant family. We decided to start fostering children. We had both worked with kids for years; we had the experience.

So, we went through the steps and became treatment foster parents, meaning we would be taking 'hard to serve' children. We would be trying to help them work on specific goal areas. These were children with much higher needs and more behavioural difficulties than most. I moved at this time from working in the group home to working in a behavioural classroom with the same agency and the same types of clients. I still work there today. So, I began fostering at home and working with kids during the day. I had no idea what a challenge that was going to be.

We knew it was going to change our lives; it would be difficult to have strangers in our home. We knew that it would require an enormous amount of time, patience and love. We had no clue that the next seven years and fourteen foster children would see some of the most trying experiences of our lives. They have been difficult, emotional and scary years; also demanding, rewarding and amazing.

The majority of the kids I cared for were teens and all but two of them were girls. They would come to us from group homes or other foster homes or sometimes right from their own families. They all came to us with a history of severe abuse. They were neglected and longed for a normal family. The trouble was, most of them really wanted their own family. They wanted their own family to be willing and able to care for them; or they simply hoped that they existed at all. This longing for real family, coupled with the abuse suffered at the hands of those same people caused them so much sadness, grief and anger. Much of the time, these feelings were projected onto us as their foster parents. We weren't their real parents, so why should they care? Why would we? It was a defensive wall they built up around them to protect themselves from further pain. We kept reminding ourselves not to give up on them; they had no one else."

Many of the kids had psychiatric difficulties and/or severe intellectual and developmental disabilities to deal with; which inevitably led to extreme behavioural problems. Dealing with disobedience, yelling and swearing, theft and property damage became part of the job. It wasn't easy, though.

Sometimes, in the group homes, angry children would react by lashing out at the staff or making false statements and allegations of abuse. Naturally, all such claims would have to be investigated and the accusation would become part of one's personal file; regardless of the outcome. When the Children's Aid investigates a foster family, they often interview the natural children, as well; which can be quite upsetting.

Although we were determined to never give up, there were certain things we couldn't tolerate in our home. If things were too severe, the teen had to go. As emotional as that could be, we had to be safe as a family. Still, we told ourselves, "Don't give up." By not giving up in these cases, we kept in contact with the kids after they left our home. We still wanted to help them; we just couldn't live with them. Those were the really hard times.

The greatest reward of being a foster parent has been the challenge of caring for a child not born to me and the chance to make a difference. All the good times have greatly outweighed the bad. My trophies are all the hugs, the letters and the thank you's; or someone who isn't my child wanting to call me mom, because they appreciate me. Those memories are a bountiful return on the investment of time and energy and emotions. The cards and letters left behind are traces of the amazing human beings that have passed though my life.

My daughter has become a rich human being as a result of her experiences with fostering. She walks tall and proud when she tells others that we help kids who don't have a mom or a dad. She is almost five and loves to brag about how many brothers and sisters she has. More importantly, the values that have been passed on to her shine through so brilliantly in her personality and her interaction with others.

I received a booklet once from one of my foster sons; I'll call him 'Bill.' Bill was extremely developmentally delayed. He was in my life for years before he came to live with me. Bill was probably one of the most severe abuse cases I had ever come across in my career as a foster parent or a child and youth worker.

When Bill first came to the agency, he could barely speak. He mostly just grunted. He had been locked in closets for long hours at a time and beaten when he was just a toddler. When he cried to be let out, his parents would just turn up the music loud enough to drown out his screams. Bill was denied his most basic needs in addition to love and nurturing.

Bill touched my heart from the beginning and for several years, I would bring him home for Christmas and other holidays, as he had no family he was allowed to visit. We grew very close.

Bill's dream was to live with Steve and me and eventually it came true.

Bill is much older now and doing well. I still look back at the letters he would write me in his broken language and feel so emotional. One such booklet he made me said on the cover, "My Book of Julie, She is so Nice to her son Bill" On the inside it read,

> "Julie loves Bill a lot. Do Julie know how mush Bill loves her. When Julie looks into Bill's eyes does it tell a stories? Julie is a hard work mom and has time to see her loveing son. I do love to you. Julie like me. Julie is one of the nice mom in the word. The end. I love you."

For a boy who couldn't write the word 'it' four years before, I knew exactly what this all meant.

I have lost touch with a few of the kids I've fostered, but I still hear from most of them. It makes me feel a little old when I hear from one or the other, telling me they just had a child of their own. When I hear about a few that aren't doing well, it makes me think, "What could I have done differently?" Then I am reminded of that mantra, "Don't give up." I change my thinking to, "Is there anything I can do to help now?"

Being a foster parent or a child and youth worker takes all the strong values and virtues that I learned from the important people and experiences in my life. Like my grandfather, my Sensei, my husband and many others. It requires patience, most of all. Willingness to learn from your mistakes and to change what isn't working is a necessary quality, as well. Gratitude, an open heart, love and determination will prevent you from giving up.

It's been fifteen years since I first walked into that group home; seven years there, eight years in the classroom and fourteen foster children later. My family and I have decided to take a break from fostering for a while. We'd like to devote a bit of extra time to our own kids while they are still young. We may foster again sometime in the future and I will continue to work with the kids in the classroom. I'm not sure I could ever really leave working with kids completely.

A year ago, I happened upon modeling. It was a bit of an accident, but something that I'm enjoying immensely. It's so different from anything I've ever done. Like everything else in my life, I will pursue it with the same passion, determination and gratitude that I have applied to all my work. I worked my first big commercial job last month and just returned from my first big photo shoot in New York.

I will be thirty-five this month. I still get scared and anxious sometimes and I still make mistakes. I still have an attitude sometimes. I even like to cause a little trouble now and then. I have done things somewhat differently than my parents and in other ways, exactly the same. I haven't changed the world, but I have made small differences. I have come a long way and have a long way to go, still. I am so thankful to everyone who has helped me and taught me along the way. There is one thing that I have learned however, all on my own. I can do anything I want, have anything I desire and accomplish anything I set my mind to as long as I don't give up.

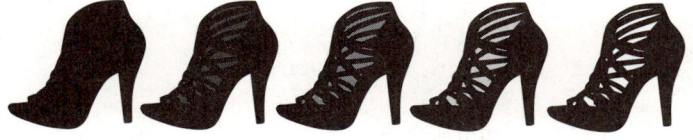

Nirvana Savoury

My mother was told that I would do great things in my life; that I was born to be a famous performer. A friend who was believed to be psychic delivered this news to her shortly after I was born. Ever since I can remember, I've loved performing; I grew up on stage. Mom was a dance teacher and as a child, I longed to be the star of the show. No matter what was going on, I had to be the center of attention.

I used to wake up early and sing at the top of my lungs; rousing my entire household. My brothers dreaded Saturday mornings, because I would sing, *See See, My Playmate*; making sure the whole house heard me. Mom recognized my love for music and performing and started my training at a young age. I started learning about ballet before I could walk; taking singing lessons at six and various other forms of dance as I grew older. Once I could watch TV on my own, I became obsessed with music videos. I would record the music videos to my favorite songs and watch them over and over again, learning the words to the song-and-dance routines. Then, I would gather a group of my friends and bring those videos to life in my living room; starring me, of course.

At the age of two, I had my first performance. It was a ballet recital. I remember stopping the show to introduce myself to the audience, "Hello. My name is Nirvana. I'm going to be a famous singer and actress!" The audience roared with laughter at my introduction as I signaled the pianist to continue the show; I was quite the character.

With three brothers (two older and one younger), I was the only girl in our busy household. My eldest brother, Tai, hated staying home to look after my younger brother and I; he only seemed to come home after school to prepare dinner for Kieron and myself. Then he would head back out to be with his friends.

My second oldest brother, Grier, was the black sheep of our family; bright, handsome, talented and stubborn. He's very stubborn to this day. But, he's managed to make life work for him on his own terms. As kids, Grier and I used to fight constantly. He felt I had to listen to everything he said; but, I too, was very stubborn. Everything my brothers tried to force me to do, I fought hard to do the opposite. In spite of that, they managed to turn me into their personal assistant. They had me do most of their chores and cover for them when they were out past curfew. Also, I primarily took care of Kieron while my brothers hung out with their friends and my mother worked three jobs. In hindsight, my older brothers taught me some good lessons: Discipline, multi-tasking and loyalty. They also made sure that I learned not to wear my emotions on my sleeve.

We grew up in a tough neighborhood; Regent Park was the first housing project in Canada. By the time I was twelve, I thought I had seen it all: Prostitutes, crackheads and drug dealers. Seeing people living in those conditions never rattled me. One thing I knew for sure: *I* would *never* live that way. I promised myself that I would make better choices.

My mother was a determined single parent. Mom did well for us by sending us to schools outside our district. She didn't want the neighbourhood to affect our lives. She always knew living in Regent Park was temporary and was determined to provide a better standard of living for her kids. It's so easy for the influences of the 'hood' to ensnare children these days. Mom wanted to make sure her kids did *not* end up being statistics. We always had new clothes, were enrolled in extra-curricular activities and frequently traveled to New York City (where I would later set the foundation for my career) to visit family for the holidays.

I had a great childhood. My mother was a great provider, despite her circumstances. Although she was a single mother, she never once complained. She always found ways to provide for us and make things work. I have learned so much from my mother; we share the same determination and ambition. I work hard and I don't settle for less.

I am very passionate about what I do. This is something all women should learn at a young age.

* * *

I continued my music and dance training by attending Cardinal Carter Academy for the Arts, the only Catholic high school for the Arts in Ontario at the time. Getting accepted into this school was a big deal for me; there were less than 35 openings for the vocal program I was interested in and thousands of students across the greater Toronto area were turned down.

My high school years at Carter were tons of fun. I met and learned from so many talented people and still maintain friendships with many of those people today. During my third year at Carter, I got pregnant by my boyfriend of two years. The pregnancy was unexpected; I was the last girl in my circle of friends that *anyone* thought would get into that situation. I had always talked about my music, my recordings and wanting to move to New York City to pursue the music deal I was going to be offered by a major label. I had my life mapped out; my goals clearly in sight. Pregnancy was the *last* thing on my mind.

I decided to have my son and it was a decision I made on my own. His father and I were together, yes, but having this child meant understanding that I could very well end up raising him by myself. We were high school sweethearts; we were in love, or so we thought. I couldn't see him leaving me to deal with this huge responsibility by myself. But, I knew anything could happen. So, when I made my decision, I understood: *This child was going to be my responsibility.*

My school's administration was very accommodating when I told them the news. I had a horrible case of morning sickness. But, I was determined to not fall behind in my studies. Up until that time, I had done well in my courses despite the fact that I hardly paid attention in class; I knew I didn't need to be in the classroom to complete my courses. My Guidance Counselor and I came up with a plan that enabled me to attend school part-time and complete my work at home. I finished Grade 11 with all my necessary credits with the rest of my class. I am very grateful for this. The teachers at Carter were awesome.

Once I got over the morning sickness, being in school part-time allowed me time to look for work. I knew I needed to be able to provide for my son; I couldn't rely on his father. Although he had promised me his support, I had to ensure that no matter what, my son would never go without. He was *my* responsibility.

It took me months to find a job. I finally landed a gig working for *CIBC's President's Choice Financial* as a phone banker for a virtual bank with no branches. I was 17 years old, making $36,000/year with full medical and dental benefits. That job was a blessing.

My life changed drastically when Jaylen was born. I was transformed from a child into a mother and I had to grow up overnight. Jaylen became my nucleus; the center of my world. Prior to my pregnancy, like most teenagers, I had given my mother a very hard time. I'd thought I was grown; thought I had seen it all living in one of the toughest neighborhoods in Toronto. Once I had my son, however, that mentality changed. I quickly realized how much I didn't know about life, myself and the world.

When Jay was six months old, I went back to school to get my diploma. I enrolled in a co-op program and got a placement at a recording studio. Jaylen's father didn't want me in the music world anymore. His exact words were, "The *B.E.T.* lifestyle is not fit for a mother." He wanted me to give up my dream of being on the stage, so I compromised. I decided to learn the dynamics of running a successful recording studio as an audio engineer behind the mixing board, as opposed to being the artist in the booth.

It didn't take long for my love of music to resurface. I was in the studio six hours a day, learning the business side of things and watching talentless people going in and out of the booth. My boss didn't discriminate when it came to clients. He was charging $85/hour for studio time and capitalized off every Tom, Dick and Harry who wanted to be a star. If they had the money to pay for the studio time, he took it.

Eventually, I started recording again. It started with my boss asking me to reference songs. Soon, I was doing some background vocals and contributing to songwriting sessions; not realizing that my love for music was simply being fed and the fire inside me was growing. Being a new mother had put my passion on a slow burn, but getting back in the music environment had given me my spark again. Within months, I was back in the studio, recording my demo.

I never actually finished high school and got my diploma. After I finished grade 12, I returned to work at *CIBC* full time. Providing a means for my family was more important than obtaining a diploma. I was only two credits shy of graduating when I left school. I was back at work full time and recording in the studio part time. I had found a balance between life at home and music; I was happy.

Jaylen's father wasn't pleased with me getting back into the music scene, however; he was insecure. He would call the studio, harassing me to come home, but as soon as I got in, he'd take off with my car until morning. Sometimes, he'd come home with some ridiculous recorded samples of his attempts to make a rap demo in his friend's home studio. He was absolutely terrible. I found it amusing that he was so against me pursuing my dream, yet he persisted in dabbling in *my* area of expertise. I never told him how I felt about that situation; I figured at some point, it would all blow over. Eventually, it did.

I was lucky to have my mother's full support when I got pregnant. Without her, I never would have been able to overcome the obstacles I've faced as a mother and performer. She continues to be my backbone and strength; she's always been there to pick up the slack. Especially when Jaylen's father decided he no longer wanted his responsibility on a full time basis.

We split up shortly after Jaylen's first birthday and a few months after I got back into the studio. We were young and had much to learn about life; we had different ideas of what life and success meant. We had grown up with two different examples. I watched my mother provide for, and raise, four children on her own. His mother had tackled different obstacles and provided entirely different examples. As a result, we defined success differently. I quickly realized I was unhappy. I refused to settle for a mediocre life. He, on the other hand, was in transition; trying to figure out his path. I had neither the time nor the patience to wait for him to figure things out. I already had a child; I wasn't about to baby-sit a grown ass man. By the time Jaylen was fifteen months old, I'd outgrown his father. I ended our relationship on December 31st, 2000. He didn't take the break up very well; as a result, his commitment to parenting our son suffered.

* * *

My career really started after I had my son. I was recording with various producers and had songs placed in movies. I traveled to New York City to meet with industry execs about recording contracts and recorded with Rodney Jerkins, one of the biggest producers in the world. Things were moving forward and it was exciting. But, nothing ever felt right.

This business is full of characters; predators. There are people who will sink their teeth so deep into you, that you are almost forced to accept the terms of their contracts when an opportunity finally presents itself. Having worked at the recording studio during my co-op placement, I had learned a lot about the *business* of music. So as a result, I turned a lot of 'opportunities' down; simply because they didn't *feel* right. I figured that if it was the 'right' opportunity, it would have happened for me. So, when I got the second call to join a manufactured Toronto girl group, I figured I'd hear them out.

X-Quisite was technically my first recording contract. I say technically because I had previously signed to a production company as a solo artist two years prior to the *X-Quisite* deal. My life with *X-Quisite* lasted all of five months. In that time, we recorded an album, shot a video and did some promotional work with light touring. Our single, *Bad Girl*, was played on radio stations across Canada and quickly climbed the Canadian charts. The music video was in high rotation and there was talk of a U.S. deal. The group seemed to be great on the outside, but there was so much going on internally between the members, the label and our 'management'. One thing I learned from that experience is that working with multiple personalities means you should expect everyone to have different motives. I'm a firm believer in loyalty and teamwork but in order for any group of individuals to succeed, everyone has to be on the same page. Considering the different agendas of the three ladies of *X-Quisite*, the production company that basically owned us and the 'wanna-be' Manager slash former exotic dancer who was manipulating us, it's little wonder the group only lasted five months. The experience was fun and I personally learned a valuable lesson: Working with people takes a certain dynamic; no matter what the commitment is between the members. After the group, I once again started from scratch; re-defining who I am as a recording artist and performer. *X-Quisite*'s music was very bubble gum. It was cool, but definitely a far cry from a true representation of *Nirvana Savoury*.

Once *X-Quisite* was over, I began songwriting with a childhood friend of mine from my old neighborhood. "Kyle" and I had done some songwriting sessions prior to *X-Quisite*, so getting together creatively was a familiar joy. We shared a love and passion for music. Kyle was extremely talented; he was able to communicate huge emotion and feeling by playing the keyboard. I admired his talent. While working with Kyle, I allowed myself to cross the business/pleasure boundary for the first time.

I had just broken up with my boyfriend of three years and music was my therapy. As a result, I spent a lot of time at Kyle's studio in his mother's basement. We created beautiful music together; music that is *still* some of my best work. Unfortunately, Kyle and I no longer talk, let alone make music together. This is unfortunate because the music he and I created was timeless. In hindsight, my mistake was simply crossing the business/personal boundary. A mistake I have vowed never to make again.

Being in a relationship in the male-dominated music world is very tough. In my prior relationships, the men couldn't handle me being constantly surrounded by successful and wealthy men. The environment played on their insecurities and lack of achievements, eventually leading to the demise of those relationships. So, when Kyle and I crossed the line, I made it clear that my interest was in the music and nowhere near any sort of romantic relationship. I was still getting over my ex and far from wanting anything serious. But somehow, that got lost in the translation and next thing I knew, I was being called 'his girl.'

Life in the studio with Kyle was magical. The music we created was great, but he was harsh and abusive. He would make jokes of my mistakes and call me names when I wasn't delivering the result he wanted. I used to laugh off his comments, but deep down they affected me so much that my already low self-esteem sunk to almost non-existent. He even tried to take the one proud moment I had from me; motherhood. I'll never forget his painful statements, "You're proud of being a single mother? That's not something to be proud of! You should be ashamed!" He put me down in every way possible. Then he would tell me *he* was the reason I was going to be successful; *he* was going to make things happen. That was his way of breaking me down to gain control.

Kyle's attempt to control me sexually was the last straw, though. His sexual preferences were incompatible with mine, to say the least. Because I loved and admired him, I agreed to try things his way; the results were painful and unpleasant for me. But, when I let Kyle know that I couldn't allow our sex life to continue in that vein, he was angry and disappointed. He refused to engage in more traditional sexual activity. Yet, he tried to convince me that I was the one who didn't love him. I stood my ground and it felt good.

After I ended the sexual aspect of our relationship, Kyle decided we needed to take a 'break' from the music. I didn't understand that because I felt it was important to keep the momentum going. He had his reasons, though and they were all about control. I was frustrated; he knew music was my outlet and he didn't care.

For three weeks, we constantly argued before we finally had a discussion about getting back in the studio. We argued for hours. By that time, we had no sex life and hardly spent time together; I didn't want to be with him intimately. I just wanted our friendship and creativity back. After arguing for hours, Kyle gave me an ultimatum; sex (his way) or no more music. I was in shock after he said that. I cried hysterically for nearly an hour. Music was my outlet, my life. Now, it was being held hostage for my body and soul; it was wrong. Music is supposed to be a beautiful thing, not a compromise. At that moment, I didn't care about the music anymore; I just wanted out.

Kyle called back. He apologized and said he was wrong for demanding such things from me. He said within a week he'd be ready to get back in the studio. I believe this was God's work. My cries were heard that day and He answered them.

Kyle and I finally completed our demo, but by then we were no longer even friends. I no longer respected him and didn't feel that he cared for me. Once the music was done, the severing of ties was mutual. My experience with Kyle is the reason I won't cross the business/pleasure boundary; not at this point, anyway. For now, dating anyone in the entertainment business is a definite no-no.

* * *

Presently, I split my time between my apartment in Harlem and my home just outside of Toronto in Richmond Hill. I've met so many people along my journey. I'm constantly weaning out the *predators,* since they never stop trying to get inside my circle. They never get very far with me and often give up after trying for long. My network consists of real people that function successfully in the entertainment industry; individuals who don't take their careers too seriously and understand that the business is very much a façade. You see, everyone in this business has a persona. A character they created for themselves that also functions as a bullet proof vest. That's the difference between Nirvanda Simm-Smith and *Nirvana Savoury.*

Nirvana Savoury is a performer and entertainer; Nirvanda Simm-Smith is a mother, a nurturer and a loving person. *Nirvana Savoury* has ring tones, a clothing line developing and an album in the works and has performed at Carnegie hall; *Nirvana Savoury* will tour the world someday soon, star in films and TV shows and will bring home the bacon.

Nirvanda Simm-Smith will raise her son, provide a loving home for her family and will change and affect lives one moment at a time.

The moment is now and doesn't require perfection. As long as you live in the moment; you are living in perfection. That is all that is required for success. My journey continues from moment to moment. I don't put unrealistic expectations on myself anymore. My only goal is to live perfectly in the moment; not chase tomorrow.

charysse robinson

"Who do you think you are, a *&#@* publicist?" my friend (and I use the term loosely) yelled over the clink of cutlery. I suppose my readily available PDA was a nuisance to her; especially considering I was doing a poor job of concealing my divided attention. I'm sure I retorted in some smart-ass fashion, but something, somewhere, clicked. That's where it all began; with a critical buddy and bad Chinese food.

X amount of time, countless sleepless nights, hundreds upon thousands of emails later and the joke's on you, my mediocre-now-acquaintance (she was down-graded quite swiftly). Here I am; successful entrepreneur and Owner of *pdaPR*.

Considering the amount of time spent laboring over psychology essays and finals during my undergrad year of university, this wasn't a path I had even remotely considered. Post-university, I worked as a counselor at a youth-support phone line until I climbed the proverbial ladder and had become the Executive Director. A large portion of my experience there involved event-planning and it was the night before one such event that my former friend started the ball rolling towards my future career in public relations.

Armed with a newly refurbished resume that emphasized what little event planning experience I had and a whole lot of attitude, I said goodbye to a promising career in Not-For-Profits and headed out to the big, bad city. In actuality, I already lived in the big, bad city and had enough experience with media and community relations, as well as networking and promotional work to put together a relatively decent CV. It also didn't hurt that I am nothing short of incredible in face-to-face interviews! One sympathetic CEO later and I was in. Well, not quite in, but somewhere just past the outer circle, I assure you.

I had written a heartfelt letter to the CEO of a downtown Toronto PR Firm, expressing my interest in public relations. This woman's own story was inspirational and I figured it would be a great place to start. She had been employed by a national media outlet and after being there for 25 years, decided to start over completely; creating her own firm from the ground up. I asked if she would be available to meet to give me any advice or suggestions in terms of how to get started in the business. She agreed to meet me at a press conference that her company was hosting.

When I arrived at the site of the press conference, I was nervous, excited and incredibly over-dressed! Amidst all of the chaos on site at the press conference, it was hard to ignore the giant, green mascot sitting by himself; uninterested in what was surrounding him. Upon closer consideration, I realized that the mayhem was not the regular preparing-for-an-event sort of pandemonium, but rather caused by the fact that most of the hired staff had not shown up. Eager to prove my worth, I used my excellent tracking skills to locate the nexus of bedlam and found the CEO I was to meet with.

As panic threatened, she put me to work. My agreed to ten minute meeting turned into almost three hours of engaging with the eager media representatives and guiding the green monster around the event. The costume eyeholes didn't match up with the wearer's eyes and it seemed like a good idea to walk him around obstacles and guests, rather than having him find them through collision. It turned out my enthusiasm and ability to roll up my sleeves, regardless of the task, made for an excellent surprise interview; I was hired on the spot!

I may have landed the Public Relations equivalent of Fry Girl at *McDonald's*, but it was a foot in the door and I was absolutely ecstatic! I loved the work I was doing and the front-line experience was absolutely indispensable. I was thrown into the industry headfirst. I worked my way up from stamping and licking envelopes and clipping newspapers and magazines to planning film screenings for festivals. No job was too big or too small. I worked fast and furiously and never said no; I was always available. I was a workaholic and not afraid to give up my personal time; whether or not I was being paid for it. Now that I had found my passion, I was determined to give it my all. I have always believed that there is no point in doing anything halfway so I continuously gave everything I had to give. Eventually, my eagerness and hard work paid off and I was being handed complete client accounts to handle.

I had been hired on a contract basis and eventually, as with all contractual work, the contract was up. While I would have jumped at the opportunity for renewal, I had been hired somewhat on a whim and now that the busy season had quieted down, there wasn't enough work available to keep me on full-time. At this point, I knew that I definitely wanted to pursue a career in Public Relations but decided to try something different and explored the route of in-house PR.

During this period, I worked at a public, partially government funded organization, as well as a privately held firm. This allowed me access to two very different work environments. I gained valuable experience writing speeches, press releases and boiler plates, pitching to media, dealing with crisis management (damage control), as well as government relations, message development, brand strategy and event planning and production.

With all of this experience, in spite of the interesting campaigns I was working on, I knew that I had not reached my full potential. I had no interest in climbing the corporate ladder in either of these work environments and I simply knew there was more to it than that. During the time that I had been working as a full time nine-to-fiver in strict corporate environments, I had also been freelancing on various PR campaigns. While I dedicated most of my day to corporate drudgery, it was my moonlighting work that truly excited me. I was working with film festivals, fashion designers, nightclubs; I had complete creative control of these accounts and was challenged on a daily basis to be more unique and innovative. I didn't want to continue to relegate my naturally artistic and creative nature to 'after work hours' and I was determined to make it my full-time work and it was from this desire that *pdaPR* was born!

I was terrified, of course; but I knew it was exactly what I wanted to do! Of course, that moment of complete freedom and liberation, with my newly acquired business license died quickly when I realized that I would have to completely give up every other aspect of my life to pursue my dream. I would be replacing a healthy and active social life, leisure time and hobbies; in effect, I would be dropping off the planet in order to follow my new path and invent my career.

I wish I could say that I didn't lose any friends; that everyone understood and supported me and it has been smooth sailing ever since. Of course, that's just not the case. Sleepless nights, skipped meals, writing press releases instead of going out for dinner or partying at the clubs, not seeing friends or family for months at a time, being rejected by companies and media outlets a couple of dozen times before my first 'yes'; all of these things led me to where I am now.

The experience of owning a boutique PR agency is truly unique in that I have one-on-one interaction with each and every client. I have found that large PR firms tend to have a formulaic approach to working with clients; assuming that the same type of campaign can be applied to every market and product/ musician/ festival or event. While in certain industries, it is very difficult for small businesses to be noticed among large multinational corporations, I am lucky that my clients really enjoy the personal touch and the fact that I am able to give individual attention to every campaign.

Of course there have been moments when I did not think it was all worth it; I even considered going back to the world of nine-to-five to regain a work/life balance and to have a stable income. But the truth is, it has always been clear to me that PR is the perfect line of work for me and entrepreneurship is my calling. For me, the stress and difficulty of all the added responsibility is definitely worth the payoff of answering only to myself (and of course, every single client). Being completely responsible for success or failure is what makes it all worthwhile for me. I have never taken a vacation since I founded the company and can't recall the last day I took off; but I am still the happiest I have ever been!

I have always enjoyed travelling; now I do it for work. Miami, Los Angeles, New York, Ottawa and Montreal are just some of the places I have visited on business. This year, we are also expanding our services to the Caribbean. The obvious drawback is that although I am in exciting cities with endless entertainment, I have little time to enjoy the sights after my work is done.

To date, I have worked with clients in film, fashion, entertainment, wealth management, health and not-for profit. Events I have worked include *Vancouver Fashion Week*, the *Toronto International Film Festival* and the *Canada Walk of Fame*. This year, I was onsite at the *Golden Globes* as well as *New York Fashion Week*.

Soon to be 25, I'm so hungry to be at the next stage of my career, that I feel like I've already wasted too much time figuring out what I want to do with my life. The truth is, I have come a long way and am truly blessed to be doing something that excites, inspires and fulfills me on a daily basis.

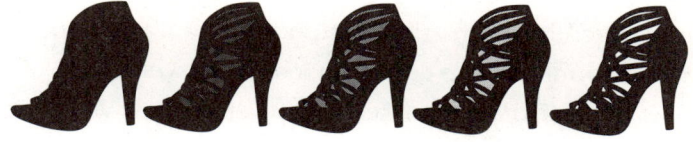

Donessa Echols

Finding My Voice

Today, I awoke hearing the words, "I love you" and realized it was my own voice. I'm still in awe every time I wake up to those words; they are proof of how much I've grown over the years. I work as a life coach, spiritual adviser, author and inspirational speaker and I love what I do. These positions have led me to create my own business. *Our Greatest Good* is dedicated to helping people reach their highest potential and truly find and follow their inner voice. My work allows me an incredible opportunity to get to know fascinating people on an intimate level. Despite their incredible gifts, these people are still searching to release their inner voice. They open their hearts and lives to me and we both heal in the process. My encouragement leads them to help themselves and by doing this, I am consistently healing myself. The most fulfilling part is knowing that the passion I have within me makes a lasting difference in the lives of others.

Although my life now consists of loving others, I didn't live that way growing up. I was raised in a home with many conflicting emotions. While my parents were good people who wanted desperately to love and be loved, they lacked the ability to express their emotions and needs. All too often, they would couple their problems with alcohol; leading to volatile and hurtful arguments. Both from troubled homes themselves, my parents hadn't yet shed the pain of their childhoods. They carried this pain into their marriage and ultimately, into our family.

My father suffered from Bipolar Disorder, a serious mental illness punctuated by extreme mood swings. The inflicted may bounce from overly energetic, 'high' or irritable moods, to sad and hopeless; then back again. They often have normal moods in between. The 'up' feeling is called mania and the 'down' feeling is depression. When my father consistently took his prescribed medication, he was wonderful and even tender. But, his medication also limited his alcohol consumption. He couldn't go for long without drinking alcohol, however, and would sacrifice his medication for drinks. To my father, alcohol provided an escape from the harsh reality of his pain. Once the arguments started between my parents, their egos would fire up and all hell would break loose until they finally broke apart. Eventually, they separated and began to move on with their lives. At least, the screaming stopped and my home life settled down; or so I thought.

Although separated, not much changed within my parents heated and emotionally charged relationship. As their child, I had begun storing up this negative energy. I constantly felt an air of uncertainty; not only with the state of my parents' relationship, but also my own life. Thoughts of suicide filled my mind; the idea was the escape from my troubled life.

It wasn't much later that I was introduced to the reality of death first hand. One night, at the innocent age of twelve, I remember chatting on the phone with a friend. Suddenly, from a back hallway of my house, I heard my mother's shrill scream, "Your father, Oh my God…"

I raced down the hallway to the sight of my mom's tear-streaked face buried in my stepdad's shirt. My stepfather was the first to speak the horrific news, "Phyllis shot your dad." Phyllis was my father's girlfriend. These words are forever etched in my mind; although the events following his death still blur together.

The graphic scenes that led to my father's death haunted me for quite awhile. Not for the first time, his girlfriend had been in the grip of a jealous rage. Previous attempts to control my father had been mere threats; but this last time had been different. That episode ended my father's life. His girlfriend was convinced that my father was going to leave her. In a moment of desperate jealousy, induced by alcohol, she walked into their room with a loaded gun and shot my father. Her first shot was aimed at his chest and he jumped up to pull the gun from her hands. In her panic, she fired the gun again, this time with a fatal blow to his head. Although paramedics tried to resuscitate him, he was pronounced dead on arrival at the hospital. After a sobering night in jail, she finally learned the consequence of her temporary moment of insanity.

After seeing my parents' love end in disaster, divorce and finally death, I ran from anything that came close to love for a long time. My anger kept building up and I didn't know how to express it. I had no idea how to let it out; nor did I think it was okay to feel such anger. I quickly came to the conclusion that love wasn't for me. But in reality, I caused myself pain because I pushed love away.

Throughout my high school years, I shielded myself from feeling any emotion. I rebelled against anyone and anything. I thought I knew it all and couldn't tolerate having someone tell me what to do. My relationship with my mother deteriorated. After another epic battle, I finally packed my bags and left home for good. At 16 years old, I bounced around many different homes, first staying with my sister, then a friend from school and finally, a friend from work. I finished out my senior year of high school crashed on her couch. Although she offered just a couch, the rent was reasonable and her generosity greatly impacted me.

The reality of paying bills and making it on my own came into focus. I stepped up to the plate by working three jobs. I went to school until lunch and then left on a work program. I worked afternoons and evenings at a restaurant and worked at a salon on the weekends. I had signed emancipation documents by my graduation and was finally free to pursue my dreams.

My dream was to sing. I applied to the Art Institute of Atlanta, was accepted and began to study Music Production. I started working as a cocktail waitress to make ends meet and slowly, my schooling was edged out of the picture. I felt my job was more exciting and it was earning me money. What I didn't realize at the time was that staying in school would have increased my pay exponentially in the long run. I surrendered my dream to my own fear of making it. I created the habit of working hard just to make enough money.

I felt restless in Atlanta and decided to move to Daytona Beach, Florida. I shared my days with the connoisseurs of quarter draft beers and shuffleboard. This was quite an educational time for me; revealing exactly what I didn't want for my life. Thinking I could start fresh with my singing career, I moved to Orlando, Florida. I began singing house music for two DJs as their vocalist. We performed at parties and raves. Our first live show was in Portland, Oregon. This was exciting to me because I was actualizing my dream to travel and sing. I even recorded a couple of records.

During that period, at around the age of twenty, I was introduced to drugs. I used ecstasy heavily for two years. Ecstasy causes a rapid release of serotonin in your brain; giving you a euphoric feeling. Because I had spent so much time focused on the pain and anger from my past, I eagerly welcomed the euphoric feeling. During that time, I experienced peace from the endless chatter in my mind. For the first time, I stopped beating up on myself. In the numbness of the high, there was no connection to judgments, sabotaging, or self-hatred; just feeling high. In those moments of drug-induced euphoria, I actually felt safe enough to crawl out of my inner shell. However, those moments were very brief, as the horrific truth of drug use became clear. I watched many dear friends ruin their lives because of drugs. Many of those closest to me lost their precious life to drugs; including the DJ of our music group. Toward the end of my use, I realized that I could experience the euphoric feelings without any substance in my body; I just needed to learn how to get there.

I stopped using ecstasy; but one of the things I took with me was the realization of the light at the end of the tunnel. I knew intuitively that this light wasn't to be found in the superficial, instant gratification of drugs. I realized there was another way to feel and that I could arrive at those feelings of euphoria without drugs or alcohol. I wasn't releasing the pain and fear that I felt; instead, I was pushing it down with the drugs and then layering more on top because of my unwillingness to face myself. I was in denial about my self and it showed in all areas of my life. I thank God that I found the intuition and strength to realize it.

After a trip to Los Angeles with a friend, I realized that was to be the next stop on my journey. I packed up everything I owned in a U-Haul trailer and headed across the country. I didn't know anyone in

Los Angeles, so after a short stay in a few local motels, I found a roommate and moved into an apartment in Hollywood, California. Again, I hustled to work as opposed to following my dream of singing. Burned out by the music business, I decided to get into acting; another way to express my creative voice.

I did a little acting and a few jobs behind the scenes as assistant to a Set Director. I got sidetracked by the excitement of city life and found myself entangled in a stormy, long-term relationship. I was searching for something, but couldn't understand what it was or how to find it. I was suffering from quite a bit of anxiety and remember thinking suicidal thoughts often. As scary as that may seem, it was familiar to me. I attempted suicide several times.

The last attempt landed me in a seventy-two hour suicide watch program. It was humiliating! The freedom I had fought my entire life to experience was gone in an instant because I had put myself in that position. Had I not come to the hospital at that time, all of my organs would have shut down. I began to question my life. How could I be so careless with my life? Why was dying the only solution I could see? I never arrived at a worthy solution because I was hearing through a cloud of doubt and depression.

An evening in October raised the stakes and deepened the emotional scars as they became physical. I was in a car accident because of my recklessness. I had been drinking with friends in Malibu and foolishly got behind the wheel of my car. The canyon roads are very curvy and visibility was poor due to unlit streets. These factors, coupled with my excessive speed and driving under the influence, created the moment of an irreversible fate. I had come around the curve incredibly fast and hit the only concrete barrier on the road head-on. The impact was so great that items in my trunk broke through the back seat; the dashboard was broken from the frame. The car was completely totaled and I was instantly knocked unconscious. I came to my senses still dazed and didn't even realize that I was in an accident. I tried to start my car and when it wouldn't start, the realization of what had happened came rushing back to me. My airbag had deployed and broke my nose in the process. My ankle was broken from hitting the brake and my wrist broke from the impact of the window. I suffered a concussion and broken cartilage in my ribcage.

Miraculously, my cell phone still worked and I called a friend who then called 911. I passed out again and like an angel sent from God, a passing car stopped to help. From what I remember of my savior, he said he too had had an accident in the same location, on the same harvest moon, several years prior. I lapsed again into a foggy state before arriving at the hospital.

After about four months of rehabilitation, I was given permission by the doctors to resume my normal activities. I began to walk the path to a new life. Just two weeks later, I was walking in a hospital parking lot and got hit by a car, which broke my other leg. I endured another five months of rehabilitation.

Since I was a teenager, I had been seeking to discover my true self; but I could never fully actualize my power. I had been running forever. Running away from the reality of my father's death; from the illusion of my mother's control; from drugs; from suicide; ultimately I was running from myself, from my inner voice. The accident and the time I spent in recovery forced me to slow down and see the power that already existed inside me. For the first time, I discovered the clarity of my inner voice. I was able to access this because I began to work intensively with a life coach.

A life coach is a person who personally coaches a client in his or her life. This partnership works to resolve personal, emotional, behavioral, spiritual and lifestyle issues. Working with my coach taught me the 'how to' of using my gift of intuition. By using some simple tools, I began to let go of the old beliefs I had about myself and my life. He helped me take complete responsibility for my life, my future and my incredible gift. I finally forgave my mother; realizing that she had done the best she could. I also came to understand that my anger towards her was just a mask hiding me from my own pain. When I unveiled this truth, I realized what an incredibly brave and beautiful woman she really is. This healed my vision of my parent's relationship as well.

Another amazing gift I received from this work is forgiveness for my dad's girlfriend. I have such compassion for her now and can only imagine what her life has been like since that day. I pray that she has forgiven herself. We are all here to learn in this movie called, "life." Learning to release resistance to anger, sadness, rage and many other emotions is to experience forgiveness and love for ourselves and one another.

Once I was able to surrender resistance to past emotions, my life changed tremendously. I learned to stop blaming other people for the things that had happened in my life. Today, I am committed to passing on this valuable lesson. I am using my inner voice to help others uncover their own talents. My life work is centered upon listening to the inner voice that is within all of us. By releasing painful emotions, we tap into our true and most beautiful purpose.

Throughout my life, whatever job I put my energy into I excelled in, but I never experienced the fullness of my talent or tapped into my greatest passions. The dread I felt for work was reflected in many other areas of my life. I was choosing work from fear or scarcity, yet was actually making things worse and I just didn't see it. Think about how much time you spend dedicated to your job, career or school. If you aren't happy or fulfilled with what you do, you're spending 40 plus hours a week feeling unhappy or unfulfilled. Multiply that by 52 weeks and then by 50 plus years! It's scary to think what happens when you say no to your true purpose. Whether you truly love to clean houses or dance across a stage, as long as you feel good about it, you're being true to yourself. Otherwise, you are creating a habit of suffering.

When I worked to pay the bills and not to feel joy and love, I was missing the real point to life. I was living in fear by thinking that I couldn't do what I loved and have all my needs met. I finally had enough courage to let that old belief go. Now I am living my dreams.

When we love what we do and we love ourselves, we shine in a way that heals the world. Why wouldn't we be provided for if we are committed to living through love? God is on our side, love is on our side and we are provided for when we surrender to living our greatest good. Why do we want the nice car, the big house, the amazing relationship and the vacations to beautiful countries? We would like to feel good and be happy. What if we began feeling good about ourselves now?

What if we went out right now and started doing things that helped us to continue the high energy of happiness? We would start to attract those wonderful experiences, places, people and things in our dreams because love attracts love. This was the most revealing eye opener on my journey and continues to be. When I remember to enjoy life or just have fun, I let go of the negative feelings. As a result, my life reflects great beauty and joy.

Throughout my journey, The Divine has provided an entourage of angels to guide me. These angels helped me see the gifts within myself and clear away the old beliefs that previously clouded my ability to recognize them. Because I felt unhappy and damaged by my past experiences, I wasn't able to see my angels. Once I surrendered, their presence was more than evident. When I left home at an early age, I had loving people to lean on, teachers who believed in me, a town that rooted for my talent, a life coach who helped me uncover my true self and family and friends who continue to encourage my dreams in immeasurable ways. I am surrounded by beautiful women whom I call my sisters and set the most amazing examples of femininity and grace. Finally, I have extraordinary clients who have become my family. I love them dearly, they love me and we are constantly letting each other know. All these people have been my support and are truly my angels.

When I think back to the times I thought I was alone, I now realize that I just couldn't see the gifts through my sadness. During my suicide attempts and drug and alcohol abuse, I was only focused on what was wrong. Therefore, more things went wrong. When I learned to simply acknowledge that I wasn't feeling happy in the moment, let go of that resistance to the feeling and learn to love myself anyway, I began to see clearly. When I suppressed my feelings to try to protect myself, I pushed myself away from all that was good and I created more non-loving experiences for myself. I am so grateful to see clearly again. I give thanks everyday for the miracles that exist in every moment. The more I see every moment as something happening *for me* instead of *to me*, my whole perspective changes.

When you love yourself completely, you will do what you love, you will choose relationships that reflect that love and accept the love you receive. Take a look at your life now and see how you can start to make changes. The happiness you seek already exists within you. Maybe you just need a little cleaning up of past experiences and beliefs. If we shift away from negative thinking, we realize that uncomfortable feelings, trying experiences, stressful jobs, lack of money and unhealthy relationships are really just red flags trying to get our attention. These experiences encourage us to face ourselves. Once we face ourselves, acknowledging the challenge, the experience that follows is ultimate peace. We realize that it's okay to feel *all* emotions and bless them as they go by.

As an adult, I still experience moments of doubt; but just like the emotions we feel and let pass through us, I release resistance to the doubt and keep going—no matter how scary it seems. Be courageous; if you're willing to take the first step, you will always be supported. Learn to listen to your inner voice for the answers. You are brave, you are beautiful and there is no one more special than you! Just as I awakened to the presence of the voice within myself, you also possess this voice. It's there inside you, humming quietly; just waiting to burst into full song, to bring fulfillment and happiness to your life.

Donessa Echols is the founder of Our Greatest Good, *a spiritual author, life coach and inspirational teacher. Donessa has accumulated many years of study alongside private instructors. Her extensive training incorporates work in the United States and the United Kingdom, including intensive study at Arthur Findlay College, an institution specializing in Spiritualism. She also serves on the Board of Directors for* Feeling Peace. *She now uses her life experiences and education to help others achieve their* greatest good.

Bobbie Phillips

Grasping a machete, I made my way through the heavily overgrown jungle, chopping the tall grass at my feet and swinging the machete overhead to pass through the thick vines. As I lunged forward to decapitate a thick, mossy branch, my right foot landed on something slimy. I immediately lost my footing and began sliding down the mountain. The jungle was drenched from the heavy tropical rains that had teemed down relentlessly the previous night; there was no way to stop my descent down the heavily mudded slope. I heard my husband yelling faintly from above, "Drop the machete before you kill yourself!" Finally, I came to rest on my drenched and muddy rear end. I sat for a moment, mentally checking that all my parts were intact. Confirming this, I stood smiling and waving the machete. I turned back toward the jungle and continued on.

That wasn't a scene from one of my action films. It was my life now; far from Hollywood, where I had made my home and living as an actress for over 12 years. I'd never really heard anything about Costa Rica and I didn't speak more than a few words of Spanish. But, there I was, on a remote tip of a rain forest jungle; having sold or given away almost every material possession I had ever accumulated. I had embarked on a new journey into the complete unknown.

One minute, I'm working in Hollywood and the next I'm building a hotel from scratch. With a few suitcases, our mountain bikes and our two rescued dogs, Rufus and Roxy, my husband, Anthony and I just stopped the world and got off. How did we get here? What made us do something so completely out of left field? As our friends and family would tell us, there were so many other logical choices if we just wanted a change

Sometimes there comes a moment in one's life when you know that the course of your life will be changed forever. In that moment there is fear and excitement, but there is also a drive from somewhere deep inside; a certainty that you have found the answer. I have come to this 'crossroads' twice in my lifetime. The first time, I was twenty-two-years old and I quit law school to become an actress.

To an outside observer, it would have appeared as though my path was a good one; I had a perfect GPA in college and job offers from respected law firms before I had even graduated. I began taking drama classes to hone my presentation skills for a career as a trial attorney. One day, out of the blue, I realized I was done; I just wasn't interested anymore. It had become the acting that made me feel alive. Just like that, I packed my bags and moved to Hollywood with no money, no prospects and no turning back.

Now, twelve years later, it was happening again. I had been fortunate to be among about 2% of the acting community that worked steadily in Hollywood. I had been able to make a living doing what I loved. I'd never had a side job, other than some modeling gigs between acting roles and I never took it for granted. I was always thankful for the work and the lifestyle full of travel and excitement that I was so lucky to have. It was also a lifestyle full of struggles and disappointments; but an exciting life, nonetheless.

But, one day, I was just finished. That same voice that had spoken to me twelve years before just said, "That's it; it's time to move on".

By that time, I was happily married to my soul mate, Anthony. We had met on a movie set in Toronto, Canada; he was my hair stylist on the film. We had a great time working together and we knew we were just meant to be. I was under contract with Paramount Studios at the time, scheduled to film the third installment in a series of television movies. It was a futuristic "female terminator" type of show and I played the title character, which gave me some nice advantages. One of those was being able to bring Anthony along to Australia as my personal hair stylist. We had a blast in Australia and some great memories that remain with us today. I've always loved filming there; it's a beautiful, happy place, in general and the cast, crew and all the Aussie's we met were always so much fun. That third go round filming "*Chameleon*" was the ultimate, because I was able to share it with Anthony.

We returned from Australia and Anthony went back to Toronto. He owned a hair salon there and was quite busy between that and film work. I continued on some other television and film roles. We worked together when we could and would meet up when one of us had time between our busy work schedules. It was getting harder to be apart, however; we decided to get married. He sold the salon to his partner and moved to California full time. The decision was made quickly and easily. This would set the tone for all decisions we would make together from that point forward.

Anthony got a job at a salon just a few minutes from our home in the Hollywood Hills, next to *CBS/Radford Studios*. He met the owners through a mutual friend. He worked there a few days a week and was also the personal stylist to a few musicians, actors and others in the business; it worked out well with our schedules.

We decided we wanted to move a little further away from the 'Hollywood scene', but we needed to stay close enough for work. We bought a house about thirty minutes north of Studio City, near a vineyard called, *Agua Dulce*, Spanish for 'sweet water.' The day we moved, in I had what some might call a nervous breakdown.

I don't know exactly what happened, but I just couldn't stop crying. I remember thinking about where I saw my life in the future; not my life with Anthony, but my career and who I was as a person. I guess, I was questioning my purpose in the world.

As an actor, there is always the question, "What will my next role be?" or, "Will I ever work again?" Such nagging doubts are common to many in the entertainment industry; it's just the nature of the business. But, this was different. I was questioning my purpose in life. Acting just wasn't fulfilling me anymore. I didn't want to be chasing roles and playing Hollywood games anymore. I was watching very talented friends in their 60's and 70's struggle at a time when they should have been secure.

Well known writers, producers and actors have to fight for respect after they've proven themselves over and over again. I had lost the energy to fight for roles or get new projects off the ground; I had just lost the passion for it. As much as I had enjoyed so much of the business, there was just so much that felt so empty and narcissistic to me. So, that's when we decided to make a change. I say *we* because I wasn't making decisions on my own anymore. Fortunately, Anthony was on board with making a drastic change; he was feeling some of what I was. He had never been impressed with the falsities of Hollywood.

Together, Anthony and I talked about the different places we could go; what we could do. We just tossed ideas around until something sounded exciting. We knew we wanted to go somewhere tropical or exotic. We thought about Australia, but it was too far away for family and friends to visit. Plus, we couldn't take our dogs because they have a six-month quarantine for animals.

Anthony mentioned Costa Rica. Neither of us knew much about it, so I immediately looked it up on the internet. Costa Rica has no army, welcomes foreign investment and has no quarantine for the dogs. It does have perfect temperatures year-round, beautiful beaches and friendly people.

"Let's check it out!" I felt hope from deep inside. I booked airline tickets for the next day and we called a friend to watch the dogs. We had only four days before I had to be back in Los Angeles for a meeting with a director; four days to decide if we were going to change our lives completely.

We checked out a few different areas in Costa Rica that left us unimpressed. We were starting to think we would need another plan. On our second day in Costa Rica, we met some people that kept mentioning a little known area called Mal Pais. It wasn't an area on my list from the internet, but we decided we needed to see it.

We fell in love with Mal Pais immediately. The beauty of the place was incredible. It was as though we had discovered a hidden paradise spread along two kilometers of the most picturesque beaches I had ever seen. There were probably 50 residents of the town at the time. It seemed that every country was represented. There were the locals, of course, but also expatriates from Austria, England, France, Italy, Israel, Belgium, United States, Canada, Germany, Holland, Argentina; you name it. Not many people, but so much culture. It was wonderful to see people from completely different backgrounds living in harmony and working together. This was it; We were moving to Mal Pais.

We flew back to L.A. and listed everything for sale. When we told Anthony's mother of our plans, she started to cry. "But, you guys have everything. Why would you move to a third world country?" That was the question every one of our friends and family members would ask. It just didn't make any sense to them. We had everything the world deemed necessary; how could that not be enough? How could we give it all up?

It's true, we had many 'things' and we were both thankful for the exciting experiences we'd had. However, we were craving something more. In a sense, we were actually craving something less; something with more depth, but freedom from the burdens and stress that can build up in today's material world. Our main and only goal was to do something that would allow us to survive. Basic food, clothing and shelter in a beautiful place sounded great to us. Just thinking about this simple life gave me joy. So, I knew it was the right decision.

So, there we were, in a Spanish-speaking third world country. We were right on the tip of a peninsula and surrounded by nature and 'real life' like neither of us had ever experienced. We were in an area that had only had electricity for the last eight years; there wasn't much in the way of technology. We were far away from the hectic, fast paced world full of text messages, cell phones and fax machines. We were in the 'tranquillo' zone and it felt great!

We decided that we would purchase a piece of property and build a few rental cabanas to pay for our existence. We found a magical piece of property that met our desires for beautiful views and privacy and bought it.

Anthony and I sat on the property for days, sketching plans until we figured we had the perfect design to go with the flow of the property. We met with several architects who, in turn, gave us staggering estimates for the cost to see our dreams turned into reality.

Undeterred, we decided to build our dream resort ourselves. We had done some home renovations that had shown us good profits in California, so we felt we were capable. However, we had never built anything from the ground up. Fortunately, Anthony comes from a family of Italian builders and architects. Although they wouldn't be on hand for the build, they gave us great advice.

Working with a local builder and an architect who would turn our sketches into proper blueprints, we began work on our dream. With only five workers and a determination bordering on unrealistic; we broke ground.

From the get go, each day seemed to bring circumstances that threatened to end the project. Just getting materials delivered was reminiscent of a scene from the *Survivor* television series. We carried bags of cement on our backs, pushed wheelbarrows of materials up mountainsides and dragged heavy machinery up a cliff with an ATV.

Incredibly and against many obstacles, we were finished in just over a year. Our dream ended up becoming more elaborate than we first envisioned. We had maintained the natural simplicity of the surroundings, while transforming our simple cabanas into an eco-luxury retreat. Our original desire of a simple existence remained intact and therefore, we really weren't prepared for what happened next.

In January 2005, we invited a few friends to stay to give us their opinion on what we had created. Within weeks, we had several celebrities staying with us. They had heard of our place through other friends and were looking for an escape prior to the upcoming Oscar ceremonies, taking place in Hollywood in late February. More celebrities followed and our little area was fast becoming the vacation home to the Hollywood elite; many of whom were nominated for the year's awards. The paparazzi followed and we turned them away; convincing them that their intelligence concerning the locations of certain celebrities was incorrect, we were merely a private home. Since nothing is visible from the entrance, they were easily convinced and went away.

Fortunately, the drama left our little town once the Oscars were over for the year. But, the area was now on Hollywood's radar like never before. Mal Pais had never seen so many rock stars, models and actors visiting at the same time. Many of the celebrities were able to vacation without any intrusion from the paparazzi. As small as the town proper is, the area is very spread out, with many remote beaches and hidden delights.

We now have many celebrities living and building homes in the area. In many ways, this is really protecting the area, since most of them buy huge tracts of land for privacy but leave most of the jungle undisturbed; there is little development. We have a bank and a pharmacy now and the roads have improved a little, but it's still remote and incredibly natural.

People ask me if I miss Hollywood or if I ever plan to go back to acting. I don't have an answer to that right now; I'm too busy living in the moment. I wake up to monkeys playing in the trees and talking to neighbors about the new fish market that opened up. I enjoy seeing guests relax and play like kids again; leaving their stresses behind as their visit unfolds.

I regularly meet people from all over the world and I find we each have a desire for a life that's rewarding and meaningful; whatever our definitions of that may be. I don't look for the answers or base my worth on external circumstances or opinions. Not that I'm immune to being affected by these things. I'm the happiest when I'm in rhythm with my inner voice. Right now, it's easier to hear that voice in the jungle; where my heart has found joy in the little things.

Hotel Casa Chameleon was chosen as "One of the Top Hotels in the World" by Conde Nast and continues to be a retreat for celebrities and couples looking for a unique escape in the jungle. Bobbie Phillips and her husband, Anthony remain in the jungle and work with several animal rescue organizations in Costa Rica.

Sitara Hewitt

"Do it, Sitara! You're so talented; you just need to include all of who you are," said Lisa. Tip #1: Having a friend who accepts you and believes in you is priceless. If you don't have that kind of friend, make it your goal to *be* that friend to someone else; in the end, you get what you give.

I was sitting in a café in India with my best friend. I had just flown there from Northern Pakistan where I'd joined my parents as they trekked through the Himalayas for academic research. I'd had months to travel because my acting career was nonexistent; I couldn't get a gig since my run at a dinner theatre show had ended. I never really minded being a struggling actor. It was more interesting than being a travel agent; which is what I had done before I quit to follow my dream.

Now I was 25 and getting a little concerned that quitting my day job to become a film and television actress had perhaps been an ill conceived plan. Just before leaving Canada, one of the most renowned acting coaches in the country had bluntly told me that I "would never play leads." True, Canada had a small industry and I hadn't gone to theatre school, but surely there was a way to turn my greatest passion and ambition into something of substance.

For the last four years, I had tried everything; acting classes, non-paying gigs, dinner theatre, commercials, etc; I was at a loss.

"Go with the Indian version of your name, Tara. You're half Pakistani and South Asian culture is starting to be so popular in mainstream entertainment." I had asked my very wise actor/director friend, Lisa Marie for her advice. Tip #2: Always use your resources.

Really? It was true that I felt connected to my Pakistani roots because I'd lived there as a child, loved the culture and spoke the language. But back in Canada, I'd always, well, hidden from my heritage. Growing up in a small, predominantly white town, I was the ethnic minority. An already shy child, I became completely introverted because of the feelings of exclusion and incidents of bullying that my sisters and I received as "Pakis". As I got older, I couldn't bear being disliked because of how I looked; or worse, how my darling mother looked. So, I avoided the whole issue as much as possible and buried that very alive part of me for many years.

I took her advice; I changed my name. Upon returning to Canada, I immediately landed a role in an English language Bollywood style film; a *lead*, no less. Sure, the role was a bit tacky and the production was super low budget, but I was learning so much and I was *acting* as a *lead* in a *movie*. My dreams were becoming realities for the first time; and I was proud to be a half Pakistani, half Welsh actress.

Immediately after the movie wrapped, I auditioned for and booked a game show. I was to be the sexy, Vanna White-style model. The name Sitara was plastered all over the show. Sure, it was a bit low-brow, aimed at a teenage boy audience, but I was getting more on camera experience and I was on TV! I made it my priority to bring class to the role and make it my own; I was promoted to Co-host in the second season. I was making it; in extremely high heels. Or so I thought.

Seven months later, I couldn't land another gig. My game show money had run out and I wasn't making enough at my bartending and hostessing jobs. I could no longer afford my beloved apartment so I moved myself and all my belongings into a room in my sister's attic. I will always be grateful for family members who supported my choice to be an artist despite impending financial ruin. I was miserable, poor and feeling like a failure once again. I had to come up with another plan. Tip #3: Never let circumstances defeat you.

My boyfriend at the time was applying to the World Wrestling Entertainment (WWE) to be a wrestler, so I decided to do the same. I threw myself into it, studying *Monday Night RAW* and creating a character. We drove down to Louisville, Kentucky in a beat-up Sunfire and lived in a motel near the WWE training facility. I enrolled in the school and went to all the events to meet the scouting agents. They accepted me and sent me on a one-week audition in Atlanta.

By that time, I'd been getting beaten up pretty badly by the practices; the bruises along my back and neck were becoming chronic and the rough lifestyle was beginning taking its toll. After my grueling audition week, I decided that I wanted to sell something more than sex and violence while brutalizing my body, so I went home to Toronto to be what I really wanted to be: an actress. Tip #4: Sometimes it takes a good honest try at something else to discover where your heart really lies.

I committed myself to acting all over again. I wanted an interesting lead role with decent pay. Tip #5: Specificity in what you desire is key. First, I needed a better agent. I submitted my package to 15 top agents in Toronto and no one returned my calls. Sitara of *'You BET Your Ass'* was not a Canadian entertainment industry commodity; she wasn't even worth meeting with. I asked a producer from the Bollywood movie if he could help me out and his agent agreed to meet with me. Tip #2 (again): Always use your resources. As an agency, she was small, but reputable. I signed with her immediately.

"I'll submit you for a sitcom tomorrow; you might be good for it," she said. The role was *Rayyan Hamoudi* on *'Little Mosque on the Prairie'*. After two auditions and a lot of coaching sessions my agent called to say I had booked the series.

That was two years ago. The show is currently in its fourth season and is seen all over the world. It is considered a 'groundbreaking' show; certainly it is the first show of its kind. My life has changed significantly and I feel very blessed. Have I made it? Well, I certainly get to do what I love on a regular basis with talented co-workers. I experience things I could only dream of in the past; for that I am grateful.

I realize, however, that even with success, there will always be challenges. I recently battled a crippling body image issue. I was able to overcome my difficulties by quitting the yo-yo dieting cycle with prayer and self-love. If you struggle with this issue, my advice is to 'love yourself fit; don't hate yourself fit.' Chew your food well; this will help you enjoy more, eat less and digest better for a flatter tummy. Learn to love exercising and energizing your body. I am happier now that I choose to look at what's beautiful about my body; not what I want to change and I am grateful for the unique miracle that is my body. I also went through a very unhealthy relationship and breakup and a chronic health issue. After working at and overcoming these challenges, I am now able to love myself and my new, wonderful boyfriend more purely and completely. I am physically healthier than when I used to stress myself into illness. Sometimes, our problems crop up to show us how we can change for the better.

As I strive to move to the next level of my career, there are still days that see me struck with fear, negativity and feelings of hopelessness. At these times, I pray; give it on up to God and refocus on just doing my best. I have a great support system of friends and family too and that helps immensely. Each night I work on breaking the habit of worry that I've had all my life by replacing it with the habit of being grateful for my blessings; big and small. I discover daily that my perspective and choice to be positive and loving make me feel successful and happy.

In an era of freedom and plenty, we get in the habit of saying, "What can I get?" Or, "I want, I want, I want." I know I did. Yes, it's important to know what you want and to go for it. But when asking for support from the universe in order to manifest your dreams, it only works if you ask, "What can I give?" No matter what you love doing; you can do it while being of some service to the world. In the end, that will be the only thing that really fulfills you. This is the most satisfying aspect of my current job. It is a huge thrill to entertain people; to make them feel okay with who they are on some level and to open their eyes to a new and unknown culture. I used to think that a job in the public eye, or 'fame' would make me feel special and happy; but it doesn't. There will always be someone more special, more beautiful, or more talented and successful than me. In the end, it's only when I feel connected to something greater than myself that I feel truly successful and motivated. What's crazy is that when I think, "What can I get?" my phone literally doesn't ring and I get discouraged and feel like a failure again. When I refocus on, "What can I give?" and look to my surroundings for inspiration, I miraculously start to get offers and phone calls and invitations to work and contribute in my field.

You can do it; whatever it is. Dream big; I always have. You can change your life and achieve great things; though it will take time and perseverance. But, why not commit to yourself? It takes just as much energy to feel sorry for yourself as it does to take the action to move forward. I've tried both and the latter is way more fun and productive. The feeling of accomplishment we experience when we succeed at something we've worked for is unparalleled and the miracles that will show up as you take control of your life will amaze you. The universe is conspiring with you. Just remember to stay balanced, work to let go of self-doubt and come from love.

Be inspired by the world around you and you will become an inspiration to all you meet.

—Love, Sitara

Jacquie Jordan

I've always liked wearing high heels; maybe because I'm five feet tall, soaking wet. The cost and quality of those high heels has definitely risen; concurrent with the ascension of my career. While I may have started my career in *Payless* shoes, I thought I had made it big when I wore *Manolo Blahnik's* to the Emmy Awards. Somewhere in mid-career, as a hard core New York City professional, I was wearing *Steve Madden*; with a sprinkling of *Nine West* heels. Now, as I settle comfortably into my ever-expanding career, I prefer to put my bare feet to the earth and feel the road I walk upon.

What would I have liked to have been told when I was up and coming in my professional game? I would have liked to have been told to "follow my bliss." I had to figure that out along the way and that mantra stays with me as I continue my worthwhile journey.

Just recently, I realized that what I do for a living; my contribution to the world, is exactly what I was doing as a little girl. However, as a little girl, I didn't know there was a name for what I was playing out and now do for a living. I believe we are intuitively given our gifts at a young age and if adults are paying attention closely, they can foster that development. If they're not paying attention, they can put the kibosh on our early instincts; we can spend a lot of time in our early adulthood trying to wander back to that space in yearning.

As a child, I loved to put on plays in my backyard with my group of little friends. We called ourselves, "The Club." Not only did I orchestrate the play, I constructed the costumes, sold tickets (even then, I knew I had a 'built in' audience) and cast the parts. Today, as a television producer who owns her own media development company,

Jacquie Jordan Inc./TVGuestpert.com/Gold Jordan Productions out of Los Angeles, CA, I'm doing exactly the same things I did as a child. Most importantly, I'm following my bliss and getting well paid for my passion.

I've always felt that I have traveled the world through the eyes of the people in the stories I've produced for television. I've helped tell the stories of hardened criminals on death row to 'A List' celebrities and everything in between. My innate curiosity, coupled with my ability to convert any story to fit varying mediums has been a staple of a career that's taken on many different shapes. In my career, I never know where the day is going to end with all of its interesting possibilities.

I believe the trap that many women fall into is trying to follow their bliss at all costs, and that's literally 'at all costs' without a concrete foundation or plan of action that grounds their inspiration to the earth or to their reality. All too often, I see young women in society abandoning their pursuits in despair; burnt out from the effort of striving to be 'Superwoman,' doing it all. In my time of mentoring women in business, I've seen women suffer in the crazy belief that we must starve for our passion or our bliss. If these scenarios don't apply to you, then kudos! Go out and support another young woman who hasn't found that out about herself. I witness many, many women starting their business with passion and ingenuity at first; whether a jewelry business, design business, home-based business or web-site business, but then peter out of passion on the climb up the mountain.

I think it's important to hold a greater vision for your potential and whatever that vision is for yourself, I challenge you to make it bigger. Then, back up and break it down into the little pieces that need assembling; somewhere along the way, the wind will blow you forward.

When I was in second grade, we were given the opportunity to sell chocolate candy bars for a fundraiser for the school. I'm not sure what possessed me, but every day after school I would sell boxes of chocolate bars to the neighbors. I sold more chocolate bars than anyone else in my class. I kept selling and soon I had sold more than anyone in the entire second grade and I kept going and sold more than anyone in the school. I didn't stop selling chocolate bars when others obviously had; I haven't stopped since, but now I sell stories in all different mediums.

My career has followed an amazing unfolding path, like the stories that I get to produce for television. It hasn't always been an easy journey. Oh No! But my reward is getting to use the gifts that I intuitively had as a child to help other people realize their potential and their dream by sharing their story and message with the world.

Kay Ann Ward

What is my story? Well, it's more of an experience and a journey. I'm not the complete me yet; there's much more to be added through the years to come, so what I have to share now is experience and the journey so far.

I'm a dancer; not a stripper, nor eye candy for videos and not a 'Hip-Hop 'ho.' I'm a dancer, a true lover of the art of movement. You can call it Jazz, Hip-Hop, Ballet or Street Jazz, but I call it dance. I'm a lover of movement and freestyle, because that's how I started dancing. When I heard music, my soul responded and my body moved freely; without any hesitation or restriction. Throughout the years, I learned specific forms of dancing and have come to respect and value those forms, but nothing brings more joy to me than moving freely.

My love for dance began when I was young. It didn't start as a result of my parents signing me up at the local dance studio; nor was I approached by an agent who thought I was the next triple threat. My love of dance came about as a result of realizing that dancing and my imagination could take me to better places. Dancing always made me feel better.

There weren't many black kids at the school I attended when I first moved to Canada. It wasn't easy for me to make friends. So, whenever I got home, I would play and pretend. One of my favourite pretend games was to imagine that I was a gymnast. I would watch gymnastics competitions on television, then stand in the living room and pretend I was running across the floor doing back flips, handsprings and cartwheels. I would also pretend I was a cheerleader.

I took my first ballet class when I was about nine years old. I never went back; I thought it was boring. My mother registered me for the community gymnastics program and I really enjoyed that. As a matter of fact, I excelled at it and my gymnastics coach suggested I continue my training at other community centres. Unfortunately, money became an issue and I wasn't able to continue. The brief gymnastics training that I had acquired helped me out throughout the years as the basics and flexibility never left my body, so I credit my gymnastics training for helping me pick up jazz and ballet.

By high school, my dancing was a lot better. I still hadn't received any kind of formal training; everything I knew and did was based on how the music made me feel and the pictures that came to my mind. I started to pay more attention to music videos so I could copy the dance moves they did. I started getting some friends together and performing dance routines at school events. It turned out the student audience liked us; we became the school dance celebrities. The teachers would ask us to perform at different events and told us how good we were and that we should keep it up.

In spite of the success of my high school dance troupe, all the dancers embarked on different career paths after graduation; including me. I never had faith; I didn't believe that dance was something that I could do professionally. I definitely got the impression that formal dance training was a must and I didn't see any dancers that looked like me. When I did see dancers who were similar to me, they were in rap and urban videos and they were not dancing the way I wanted to dance. I did *not* want to be a video 'ho. That was the terminology used and I wanted to stay far away from that.

I really didn't know where to start. The passion still lived in me; everyone who knew me was always asking me if I was going to pursue dancing. I had a high school teacher who wanted me to teach Hip-Hop dance to adults at one of Toronto's finest universities, but I turned her down every time she asked; I didn't think I could do it.

When I checked the college requirements for dance, I discovered that a background in ballet or performance was required. I was a young girl who loved to dance freestyle and knew deep in my soul that I could do it, but I didn't think it could actually happen.

After convincing myself that I couldn't do it, I took the two-year Social Services program at George Brown College. While attending, I tried a few dance ventures. I danced at the annual showcase with another dancer. The audience enjoyed it; I also did a solo the next year.

After I graduated, I started working part-time at a residential group home. I liked it; I enjoy helping others. However, I realized that if I wanted to be happy, I have to live a truthful life and love what I do; I'm no good to society or myself if I'm living a lie. So I decided to cut back on my work schedule and concentrate on dancing.

It was in this frame of mind that I went to my first audition. I was scared out of my mind. The audition was for *DLM Dance and Entertainment Company*. They needed dancers for various events and they also needed dancers to learn choreography for particular events.

After the audition, I thought, "Am I going to get a call back?" Two weeks went by with no call back, so I was convinced that I didn't get the part. In the third week, I got the call from *DLM*, but it wasn't for the choreography section. They wanted me to model and Go-Go dance. I thought, "Yuck, I don't want to do that." But I knew I needed to get in, so I took it.

At the event, I was asked to Go-Go dance to rock and roll and other music that was out of this world. I went up on the platform and I danced my heart out. I knew that this was an opportunity to show others what I could do and that's what I did.

The owner of *DLM*, Shawn Cuffie, was impressed; he continued to hire me for future dance jobs. I also auditioned to teach a dance hall reggae class at *Street Dance Academy*, I got that job also. The owner liked my style. I was the first dance hall reggae teacher the studio had. In many ways, *Street Dance Academy* and *DLM* hold a special place in my heart. Those places gave me my start and I appreciate the exposure the owners gave me.

However not all was well. Although I was strong in freestyle, I had a hard time picking up choreography. I took all the drop-in classes I could find to improve the pace that I picked up dance moves and to get better as a dancer. I did every performance I could so that I could show others what I enjoy doing.

I remember one of the shows I had done. I was so excited to be working and getting paid. I showed up to rehearsal on time and ready to learn. It turned out that was one of the worst rehearsals I ever had. The choreographer made it clear that I wasn't at the same level as the other dancers. I picked up the moves slower than the other dancers, because I wasn't used to learning choreography. I remember fighting back tears throughout rehearsal. Afterwards, the choreographer came up to me and said, "Don't let me get to you; just work harder." Those words made me feel a little better. I told the choreographer that I really was trying; that I could dance, I'm just a better freestyler than I am at picking up choreography. I went home and cried my eyes out.

I've never regretted how that choreographer treated me, because she gave me so much fuel to push myself and get better. I realized at that particular rehearsal that if I wanted to work at a professional level, I was going to have to develop a thick skin and work my ass off. So, after thinking about it, I knew I had to continue training and not let things get me down. I knew I was a good dancer and I could do it. So I started training in ballet and jazz to compliment the Hip-Hop and freestyle.

By this time, I was experiencing financial difficulties, as well. I wasn't working full time and all the money I had was going toward my training. I also noticed that no one was asking me to be part of their showcase. So I entered a few showcases by myself and danced solo. I started to become self-efficient. I learned that the industry I've chosen is very insecure and superficial and it has nothing to do with who I am as a person.

My attitude changed from, "Pick me, pick me." To, "I know I can do this. I'm good and my time will come; I don't know when, but I trust and have faith because I've felt this way since I was a kid." I love dance too much to let the opinions of others determine my destination.

With my new attitude, I got better. Choreography isn't much of an issue anymore. I'm still challenged every now and then; depending on the choreography and the choreographer. But that's what dancing is all about; sometimes you get it and sometimes you don't. It means you're learning. When my attitude changed, I noticed a shift in the attitudes of others. I noticed that more opportunities came my way; I met some great people; leaders, dancers and choreographers. I also met people who would pretend they cared for me, when I knew they really didn't. I know they speak ill of me and I feel the negative energy when they come around, so I've learned to stay away from that type of negative energy and only surround myself with goodness and positivity.

I've taken the driver's seat with my career; I've decided to trust faith and go. I may hit the ground hard at times; but I have to try. When I look back at the path that's been provided to me, I'm not upset that I didn't start training at three years old or that an agent didn't approach me to be a triple threat. Everyone has their niche and their path and this is mine. I'm able to treat others with respect. I still want to help others; just now, I want to incorporate dance into the picture. I've learned through dancing and training that fitness is something that I enjoy and I now plan on getting my Fitness instructor certification.

I still dream of dancing on a big stage and going on a world tour. I believe it will happen; I don't know when, but I'll continue to grow, perfect my craft, learn and be a good person so that when the time comes, I'm ready.

That's my journey so far. I feel good that I'm on this journey and I try to enjoy each experience as it comes. Who knows where I'll be five years from now? I'd like to be the owner of my own business, tour the world, meet great people and be at peace; continue to bring movement to life, be with family and friends and have good health.

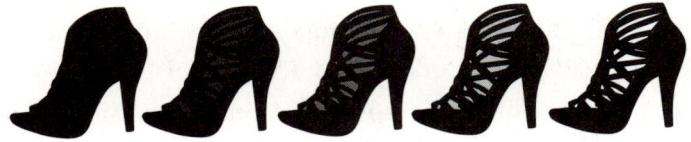

Lina Policaro

While other kids my age were busy worshipping *N.K.O.T.B* (*New Kids on the Block*, for the unfamiliar), I had my own fascination with another 90's acronym: *D.K.N.Y* (*Donna Karan New York*). Fashion was a major part of my life. My grandmother was a seamstress, my mother worked for *Estee Lauder*'s head office and I would follow somewhere in their footsteps one day; I just knew it.

At nineteen years old, I was eager and willing to do whatever I could to succeed in the fashion industry. In order to obtain my BA in Fashion Communications at Ryerson University, I was to complete an internship within a fashion-related company; 400 hours of unpaid labour. Just getting a placement was not an easy task. I emailed several people, trying desperately to get my foot in the door; any door. Ideally, I dreamed of landing an internship assisting some glamorous fashion stylist; as I hoped to one day pursue a career in styling. I wasn't exactly sure where my BA would take me, but I knew one thing—I had an overwhelming love, or sick obsession as some called it, for clothing, accessories and European designers.

Through persistent emailing, a PR agency finally tossed me a bone by referring me to some local artist management agencies. Who knew such agencies existed? A talent agency whose clients were stylists? This was a brilliant concept to me; it made perfect sense! I knew I had to somehow maneuver my way into one of these companies and land an internship. I contacted a couple of the major reputable agencies with a one-line email: "I need to complete 400 hours of unpaid internship. I am available everyday and eager to work." I knew someone would bite; I was basically marketing myself as 'a slave with a smile.'

Within ten minutes, I had received a response from one of the agencies, asking me to come in for an interview at week's end.

I began my first internship the following Monday. I had the privilege of spending four days per week, from nine to five, doing filing, running errands, making photocopies, arranging portfolios, updating the entire 5000 name database, cold-calling and doing whatever the owners and other agents needed me to do. I commuted an hour into the city every morning and while others may have whined about the mundane work; I loved it! I really did. I was grateful to have landed an internship at a company that interested me.

My hard work and dedication seemed to pay off. By the time I had completed my entire 400 hours, my bosses offered me a part-time paid position while I completed the remainder of my third and fourth year at Ryerson. Between school, work, essays, exams and my long commute into the city, I didn't have much of a social life, but I was grateful for my entry-level position into the fashion world, nonetheless. I felt like the geek who had finally made her way into the cool clique. While most of my friends were still working retail, trying to solidify a 'real' job for post-grad, I was working for the largest stylist agency in Canada. At 19 years old, I was already attending *Toronto Fashion Week*, private soirees and large charity galas. I even had opportunities to visit music video and commercial sets, as well as glamorous fashion editorial photo shoots. On top of all that, I was working for two amazing individuals, who taught me everything from business operations to life lessons. They were my mentors; they took me under their wings and helped me grow. Most importantly, they believed in me and gave me a chance.

By the time I was 21, I was working as a full-time agent and loving my job. I still had the same keenness and ambition I had started with as that wide-eyed intern. Everything was still new and exciting. By 23, I had even appeared on a few episodes of a nationally aired plastic surgery show, where I acted as the fashion industry commentator. I continued my career as a booking agent until shortly after my 24th birthday. It was then that I came to the realization that, as much as I loved the environment and all the agents and stylists I worked with and mainly my employers, I had grown comfortable and no longer found it challenging.

I immediately began perusing the internet, thinking it would be great to land a job with an agency in Los Angeles or New York City. I applied for various booking agent positions; more out of fun than from any expectation of a reply. After all, I was still quite young and lived in Canada. However, within an hour of sending out my resume, I received a call from the owner of an agency in California, who was looking to hire a managing booking agent with experience in stylist representation for her New York City agency. I was in shock; she had contacted me so quickly. We chatted for about 30 minutes. By the end of our conversation, we had arranged that I would meet her for an interview in New York City on the following weekend.

The woman I was meeting had pushed my interview back because she was running late. So there I sat, awaiting her arrival, sipping sparkling water; although I really craved some wine to take the edge off. Finally, 'Adrienne' arrived. She began by asking me about my work experience, then she drilled me with numerous scenario questions, like, "What would you do if a stylist blamed you for not working?" I answered all of her questions so well, I even surprised myself. As the interview was coming to a close, Adrienne leaned in toward me and said, "If you are good to me, I will help you. If you cross me, I will make sure you never work another day in this industry." I was stunned. Did this woman just say that to me and close her remark with a smile comparable to the Wicked Witch of the West?

Nevertheless, four weeks later, I was living in Chelsea in my new apartment. Not really new, rather old and rundown but hey, it was New York City and I was ready to embark on my glamourous new career in Manhattan. I was working in the fashion industry.

The agency was a mess; a complete disaster. After being accustomed to working at an agency that was run like a well-oiled ship, it was a shock for me to find myself in an agency contained within a 75 square-foot room within a photography studio. There were no other employees except for my assistant, who was a student at the Fashion Institute of Technology. There was no database, no office stationary, no laser printer and no functioning company website. It was an absolute mess. Michelle, the woman who had run the office prior to me, had vanished; with no indication of why she left or where she had gone.

I had a lot of unanswered questions when I started, but as a sponsored Canadian working in the States, there is a tendency to feel indebted to one's sponsor. Always an optimist, I made the best of the situation. I made sense of what I could; I met with each artist to learn about their work, their goals, their likes, their dislikes and so on. It was like starting a new agency from the ground up. I hadn't expected it to be like that when I took the job; but I'd wanted a challenge, right? I guess I should be careful what I ask for.

Months went by and the holidays were approaching. New York City was amazing. I'd made a ton of friends and was experiencing the most amazing nightlife and culture. Socially, my life was wonderful. The artists I worked with were great too, but as confused as I was about how the agency operated.

Adrienne was rarely truthful with her talent. She would avoid their phone calls and duck their questions when they'd ask why the website wasn't functioning after a year of being 'under construction.' I'd end up dealing with everyone; coming up with excuses and assuaging their frustrations. By this time, Adrienne had grown dependent on me for many things, from writing emails for her and booking jobs for her talent in California, to arranging her vaccinations for her Balinese quest for spirituality. As time progressed, the requests became more ridiculous, but I bit my tongue and continued to fulfill her demands. I had my hands full; however, I was also maintaining the artists' careers and schedules. I was only one person and Adrienne refused to hire another agent. My FIT intern was only capable of so much; between his schoolwork, part-time Barney's job and the internship.

In December of that year, a recruitment agency contacted me, offering a position as an agent at a large New York based photography agency that housed a stylist division. When Adrienne discovered and sabotaged my opportunity through reading my email, I knew that our relationship couldn't continue much longer.

The situation continued to deteriorate after I returned from my

Christmas holidays. Adrienne's requests grew increasingly unreasonable and I found myself refusing to carry out demands of a questionable ethical nature. I had never worked for anyone like that. It wasn't how I was taught to be an agent. The negative energy was too much and I feared it was beginning to affect me. I wasn't about to compromise myself as a person.

I stuck it out for another six months longer; mainly because I was locked into my apartment lease. Finally, the deadline I had imposed upon myself to quit had arrived. I called Adrienne and told her I was relocating back to Toronto; giving her 3 weeks notice. Well, as you can imagine, she did not take it well. But I was unaffected. Nothing she could say to me could convince me that I wasn't doing the right thing. As hard as it was to quit and leave the city I had grown to love, I knew I couldn't continue working at a job that I dreaded facing every morning.

It's true what they say - what doesn't kill you makes you stronger. Every bump in the road, every high time, every laugh and every tear taught me something. My experience in New York is one I wouldn't trade for the world. I learned things about myself and life that no person, book or course could have ever taught me. The job was both terrific and torturous. On one side, I was working with some amazingly talented and creative stylists; a lot of whom I developed friendships with. I had amazing clients, from *Steven Meisel* to *Vogue*, to *Calvin Klein* and *Mariah Carey*. On the other hand, I was dealing with an extremely insecure woman who always saw the worst in people. A mentor of mine said, "Imagine what a terrible world it would be if you only chose to see the negative in people." People like that exist and everyone, I believe, will encounter them at some point. The important thing is to learn that positivity and optimism comes back around. At the end of the day, it is our attitude that controls our lives.

After leaving New York City, I relocated back to Toronto with the intent of working in the music business. Needless to say, I felt I had had enough of the fashion industry. I wanted a new and challenging career that would expand my horizons. Working behind the scenes in the music industry had always been of interest to me; I had already worked with a lot of high-profile performers in music videos and magazine shoots in my fashion days. I decided that with all the experience under my belt, I could afford to be selective in my job hunt. After all, my happiness and personal fulfillment were the most important factors to me in a new career.

After many job interviews, recruitment agency meetings and after surfing numerous career websites, I came across *the* perfect job; marketing major concerts for large venues in Toronto. The process for landing this job was difficult, to say the least. There were over 200 applicants. I had been shortlisted to the final six applicants and the interview process required a phone interview, personality test, as well as putting together a major marketing plan to be presented to the company's executives. After a month of work, I received a phone call offering me the position. It took all my might to refrain from screaming into the phone receiver, I was so thrilled!

I have been at the job for over six months now and I have never been happier in my life. I work with major concert promoters, media companies and world renowned performers; doing everything from media buys to facilitating backstage 'meet & greets.' My boss is amazing, so are my coworkers. I wake up every morning looking forward to going into the office. My days are constantly filled with laughter, along with the many daily challenges that keep the job interesting and new. My hardships, struggles and numerous experiences have gotten me to where I am today. There are no negatives in life; only *challenges* to overcome that will *make you stronger.* At only 26 years old, I have now been fortunate enough to truly experience the adage, "If you *love your job*, you never will *work a day in your life!*"

Katrina Campins

At times, I wonder if wearing high heels since the age of three has changed my perspective on life. At 5'11", I stand taller than the average man and woman and with 4" heels a staple of my wardrobe; I would say my view of the world is closer to that of a 6'3" quarterback. I definitely don't fit the profile of a quarterback, but I certainly play by the same rules when it comes to my life and my career. I may wear *Christian Louboutin* heels and strut to meetings like a model on the catwalk, but when it comes to business, my mind works more like that of a man than a woman. It's easy to judge a book by its cover and expect a woman like me to use sex to sell, but when people see me in action, they can do nothing more than respect me for my abilities as a businesswoman.

I have always believed that in business, being a woman can actually work to your advantage. By learning to strike the right balance between femininity and respect, a woman can rise to the top of any company. With my entrepreneurial spirit, I made it a lifelong goal to start a company that would stand out among the crowd. I ensured that my company would succeed by applying good business ethics and developing a strong network of relationships. My greatest achievements, such as owning my own company, selling $400 million in real estate and having a powerful network of clients, all by the age of 29, weren't achieved by looks and intelligence alone. Passion, professionalism and integrity are the driving factors to my success; without those and the love and support of my friends and family; I would have failed a long time ago. My story may already be one of success, but I have high aspirations and I intend to continue pushing through and defeating all the odds.

There have been no shortcuts in my journey to this point. It began on October 22, 1979, in the brilliant city of Miami, Florida. I grew up as a privileged child in a household where my parents instilled the importance of creating my own destiny. Most people never realize that I am born to Cuban parents; parents that left everything in Cuba in pursuit of a life of freedom.

The women on my mother's side of the family, particularly my grandmother and mother, heavily influenced me to be a strong woman; very atypical from the Latino stereotype of catering to men and being a woman of the house. Truth be told, I am not subservient to men, nor am I very domestic. My grandmother fit this role well in Cuba, as she was married to a prominent doctor from a good family. She was preoccupied with raising her three young daughters in the grand era of Cuba until the successive catastrophes in her life of her husband's sudden death in his early forties and Castro's rise to prominence. Shortly after she was widowed, my grandmother managed to leave Cuba and settle into a one-bedroom apartment on Miami Beach with her three young daughters.

Adjusting quickly to the realization that she couldn't focus on the past or what should have been, my grandmother was determined to show resolve to her daughters. She worked two jobs in factories; a demeaning reality given her prominence as a grand dame in the golden era of Cuban society. She had no functional job skills and didn't speak English, so she had to do what she could to provide for her young family. From the age of ten, this was the environment in which my mother was raised.

In school and growing up in general, my mother always made my younger sister and I believe that we were much smarter and more well-rounded than either of us probably were. She instilled such confidence in me that I actually believed what she told me; which is comical when I look back on it. However, I will readily admit that the constant support and tough love I received from my mother is probably the largest single factor that shaped the foundation for my success in school and the business world. It wasn't until a few years ago that my mother admitted that she didn't actually believe I was the smartest kid in the class...

As I entered college at the University of Miami in 1997, my high school sweetheart and soon-to-be husband and business partner (we have since divorced, but remain business partners) and I began to develop an interest in real estate. At eighteen, we flipped our first real estate contract; even taking the client to a fancy restaurant for drinks, hoping that we wouldn't be carded for being underage. I obtained my real estate license that year and began trying to make some money as a real estate agent while I attended college. At that time, my priority was to obtain the highest marks that I could and I graduated in four years with honors and a 4.0 grade point average. In reviewing my transcript upon graduation, my boyfriend commented that he couldn't believe how many A pluses I had obtained in spite of not having any real incentive to achieve an A+ over an A. I just had a certain drive to be the best; a tribute to my mother, I suppose.

By the time I graduated from the University of Miami in 2001, I had notched three years of real estate brokerage experience under my belt. Beginning by helping friends with rentals at a small brokerage, I ended college by closing my first transaction above $750,000 and being employed by the top brokerage firm in Miami; Wimbish-Riteway Realtors, an exclusive Sotheby's affiliate and later acquired by Coldwell Banker.

I decided to pursue a career in real estate on a full-time basis, despite knowing that I didn't need a college degree to be a realtor. However, I knew that I loved the interaction with people and thanks to a summer internship at an advertising agency, I also realized that I couldn't work for anyone else; I don't like being told what to do and I like to set my own course.

While at the University of Miami, I was fortunate enough to develop friendships with some football players who later went professional. Due to their friendship and trust, one of them asked me one day to assist him with a real estate purchase in Jacksonville. At that time, I felt that although I didn't know the market in Jacksonville, I could be of some use to my friend as a sounding board and objective advisor.

Once there, however, I quickly realized that my friend was being taken advantage of by a local builder and that the builder thought I was a young groupie tagging along for the day. Well…the builder never saw it coming when I spoke up, took my friend out of the builder's house and never looked back. I realized I could develop a niche market by helping athletes with their real estate needs and by acting as their trusted real estate consultant. This laid the foundation for what is now *The Campins Company's Sports & Entertainment* division.

It was always my dream to make a big splash and do great things in business. Of course, at 29 years of age, I acknowledge that I still have a long way to go in the business world. I suppose that my first big life-changing break came when a friend of mine read about a new reality television show that Donald Trump was producing. We spent a day videotaping some of the property that I handled and my friend sent the video to the new show's producers. I was selected to be a contestant on the first season of *The Apprentice*. At first, I actually declined the opportunity to appear on the show, but was persuaded during a three-hour meeting with the producers. Looking back, it was an easy decision to make, but my first concern was that taking a two-month hiatus with no communication with my family or clients while I filmed in New York City would be a setback to my career. However, I ultimately decided that forcing myself to move outside of my comfort zone and potentially develop new skill sets and contacts could indeed be a great adventure. Not to mention, regardless of the outcome, I knew that this would be a fantastic life experience.

I managed to prove myself and win 'The Donald' over; up until the final episode. But my involvement with *The Apprentice* turned out to be an experience that surpassed anything I could have imagined. First, I got to live in New York City for two months; a dream of mine from an early age. I also learned many lessons from the other contestants and Donald Trump; the most important of which is the power of branding. Donald Trump is a branding expert; someone who strategically places his name on anything and everything and gets paid indescribable amounts of money to do so. As such, a major focus of mine has been to create a brand around myself and my name. I have learned that the most valuable asset is intangible, a strong brand; this is perhaps the most important indicator of success. Of course, a strong brand doesn't exist without a top-notch product or service.

After my appearance on *The Apprentice*, I didn't actively engage in real estate brokerage for about a year. Instead, I made the decision to focus on building relationships with as many people within the sports and entertainment industries as I could. Anyone in a service business is first and foremost in the business of building and fostering enduring relationships. What this means is that forming strong relationships becomes the basis for your business success; eventually sourcing referral business from your own network. Part of my strategy for doing this involved consciously extending my fifteen minutes of fame, eventually landing a corresponding assignment with ESPN's *Cold Pizza*. Not only did I make great contacts there, but I also got to meet many athletes and their families. I spoke at many leadership and real estate conferences around the country to continue to make a name for myself as a top-level real estate broker. I didn't sleep a lot that year and I didn't spend a lot of time in Miami, either. However, the hard work I strategically put in to develop relationships within the industry turned out to be a great use of my time and energy. That was an example of taking one step back to take two steps forward.

Once I had networked and built relationships around the country, I sensed that the time was right to transfer my new contacts into real business. I couldn't go on networking forever by being the girl from *The Apprentice* and I knew that I had to start shifting away from that label to one of a powerhouse real estate broker. It was at this time that my then-husband and I decided to start our own real estate brokerage company. This would allow us to make a big publicity splash and also to create our own brand. So, naturally, with me being as comfortable as I am in the spotlight and having the desire to create my own brand, we named our new company *The Campins Company*.

Starting up a new real estate brokerage company has been done by people all over the country. However, it is a business that demands that one stand out from the sea of competition and top notch service. My real focus has always been to build a brand that one day I could leverage into other industries. Keeping that in mind, we had to figure out what message our brand would convey to our clients and prospective clients. We developed a business model wherein we would target the luxury real estate market as well as the sports and entertainment industry. In addition, because of our clientele and the level of trust and management involved, we also decided that we would take on a nationwide focus within our Sports & Entertainment division. It was just as important to develop a logo and an image that would communicate this accurately. I went through several graphic designs until we came up with the perfect logo for our new business. When I finally found the right design, I knew it was the one as soon as I saw it; I felt it. I have always 'listened' to my gut and it invariably turns out to be right. In the instances where I haven't 'listened' to my gut, I have always realized belatedly that I should have done so.

I am a perfectionist. I had the perfect logo and was ready to officially launch *The Campins Company*. Being a very hands-on person, the hardest part was allowing other people to carry out certain duties. It has taken me years to realize that I have to learn to trust others and focus on where I add the most value. I know that my value is in bringing in business and negotiating transactions. Of course, the second-hardest thing about starting a business is being able to assemble, develop and retain the right team. The only way to do that is to listen to feedback, accept constructive criticism and communicate openly. It is very difficult to learn to accept constructive criticism when you are a perfectionist, but to be successful you must humble yourself and acknowledge that you aren't always right. You must define roles for your team members and trust them to carry out their assignments. If performance isn't there, you must be up front about it and nip it in the bud.

I have also learned that worrying is the most useless consumption of time and energy that exists. I started a business because I had confidence in myself and a business plan. There is plenty to worry about when starting a business and running a million miles per hour. Instead of worrying, I try to always focus on maintaining positive energy. I strongly believe that one cannot change what happens in the course of daily life, but one can certainly control one's attitude in dealing with adverse situations. I also believe that positivity begets positive results and that negativity and worry will only create more negative situations. Most successful entrepreneurs and businesspeople are probably true Type-A personalities. However, these are typically not the type of people that have tremendous patience or that are necessarily cognizant of maintaining a positive attitude at all times. It is fundamentally important to be focused on remaining positive; often it is the small items and stresses that occur on a daily basis that can sap one's energy and ability to remain focused on the larger goal or task at hand.

In tough economic times, it is all the more important for entrepreneurs to remain confident in their business plan and not allow worry to seep in. It is also an opportunity to re-visit one's business plan to make adjustments, such as cutting costs or identifying new ways to make money. In my business, I have continued to focus on relationship building. While it takes money to travel and attend events or meet new people, I also believe that the opportunities to forge new relationships when times are tough are tremendous. When everything is rolling along, people are not as motivated to look elsewhere or form new contacts. However, when business-as-usual gets shaken up, it creates an opening to position yourself in front of your target if you are confident and able to showcase how you can add value to that relationship. As such, my new business development budget has not changed, but I have cut other expenses that may not contribute directly to new business or profitability. The way I see it, I am glad that these tough times really spurred me to focus on every cent that goes out the door. I have now cut costs that I will never bring back on and that will save me a lot of money in the future; whether the economy is good or bad. Again, this is an example of finding the positive silver lining in the trough of a cyclical real estate market and faltering economy.

While real estate is certainly my passion, I have forged my career based on my own self-confidence and development of my brand. I have always stayed true to who I am and haven't felt the need to conform to certain pressures; such as wearing a business suit. I love fashion and self expression; I love being young. I love having people tell me I am so much nicer than they had imagined and I love making a splash. I also love wearing high heels in just about any setting! In fact, I believe that my fashion sense and style actually set me apart from the masses and allows my true personality to shine. I have always felt that many women are scared to be themselves in business settings and lack the confidence to achieve greatness. As I have built and continue to build my career, I seek to serve as an inspiration to women. I am a living example of someone who has confidence in herself, has a passion, has set achievable goals and who works her tail off. I really believe that an amiable woman who is good at what she does can use her femininity as an advantage to separate herself from the masses.

In giving lectures and speeches around the country, I am constantly approached by women who have many questions for me about being successful in business. The realization that I am looked up to by many has slowly created a deep interest (dare I say, passion) in my ability to help women and serve as a role model to women entrepreneurs.

I believe that every successful woman must continue to evolve in order to be successful in business; as well as in life. Life is a balance between work, relationships, spirituality and health. Women have the added stress of also trying to be the principal homemaker in many traditional relationships. I readily admit that I do not yet lead the balanced life that I envision myself leading. I tend to work too much; to the point that I sacrifice other elements of achieving a full life balance. The first step in achieving balance is to acknowledge which sphere you are lacking. It then takes a conscious effort to change. I hope that many of you can follow your bliss and create your own destiny. Anything is possible—you just have to want it and believe it!

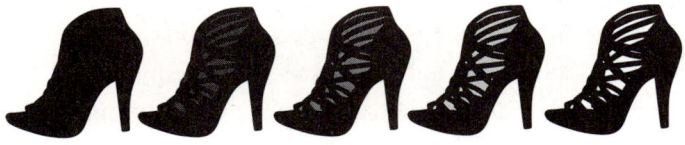

Nimisha Raja

When I was approached to write a chapter for this book, I was actually quite surprised. I had been spotted being interviewed on Rogers TV's *A Greener Toronto*, talking about the ills of factory farming. I was surprised because I didn't really consider myself as 'making it' yet, let alone in high-heels; I've been wearing flats for 98% of my waking hours for the past fifteen years. But after some reflection, I can say that yes, I've 'made it' on several levels, but still have a long way to go. Quite honestly, I don't think any of us ever really arrives at a destination that defines having made it. We can use societal norms, our own values and cultural background as guidelines for indications of success, but ultimately, I think we all just keep growing, learning and changing.

For me, this growth process continually changes my definition of success. When I look back over my life, I can see that at various defining moments, I was successful. Quite often, I was successful despite some overwhelming odds stacked against me. Luckily, I was pretty much a straight 'A' student throughout grade school and high school, as my parents instilled in me a value for education and a strong work ethic. My parents also raised me as a lacto-ovo vegetarian, emphasizing that we don't need to kill for food and teaching me reverence and compassion toward all forms of life. That value not only stayed with me, but has grown into a burning passion over the years. I've never eaten meat in my life and I dropped eggs and dairy from my diet 12 years ago, favouring a vegan lifestyle. This has played a huge role in defining who I am today. It's also helping me create a new career for myself and is the reason I was being interviewed on TV. But, I'll backtrack, so I can explain how I got there.

My dad left home when I was fourteen, after a bitter divorce from my mom. In 1977, alimony or child support payments weren't enforced by the courts as rigorously as they are today; which meant that I learned to fend for myself at an early age. I began babysitting extensively; not just the odd evening or weekend, but a steady, five-day-a-week job that brought in enough cash to pay for all my school activities and even some clothing.

I would get up early enough to get ready for school, then show up at my babysitting job next door at 7:30 a.m. It was my responsibility to help pack the two kids' lunches and walk them to school before 9:00 a.m. I picked them up after school at 3:30, walked them home and looked after them until their mom returned at 6:30. I usually also had evening and weekend babysitting jobs to supplement this weekday income, so I could save for university. It was abundantly clear to me that there was no way my mom would be able to afford tuition fees; she was having enough trouble putting food on the table and paying rent. Thank God for my older brother who, while attending school full-time, worked a night shift job, so that we wouldn't be evicted and wouldn't have to suffer the indignity of receiving welfare benefits.

The summer after my dad left, I realized babysitting money wasn't going to cut it for tuition fees. I begged my mom to help me get a job at her factory. I was fifteen, which was underage, but would be sixteen later in the summer and I reasoned that was close enough for factory work. She talked to her boss and he agreed! I was the happiest fifteen-year-old when I got the news; not realizing how exhausting the work was going to be. But I didn't complain. It was money and we needed it. Summer ended and with it, the then well-paying $3.50/hour factory job (by comparison, babysitting rates at the time were between 50 and 75 cents an hour). I was determined to get something better, now that I was 16 and legally entitled to work. However, there was a stipulation. Despite our desperate need for money, my mom wasn't exactly thrilled about me working while going to school. She thought my grades would suffer. So the deal was, if I got a part-time job, I had to keep up my grades or quit the job. I agreed and managed to secure a cashier's position at a nearby grocery store. I started at minimum wage ($2.85/

hour), but quickly climbed to much better rates, as the policy was to increase pay automatically every 3 months. I kept that job throughout high school and university and it did for the most part pay for tuition and books. I did have to get a couple of small OSAP (Ontario Student Assistance Program) loans, but repaid those within 6 months of graduation to avoid interest payments. I graduated with a major in economics and thought I'd climb the proverbial corporate ladder on the road to conventional success: money and a title.

A secret dream at the time was to be able to take a year off working to travel. Many of my classmates had parents with the financial means to allow them to travel throughout Europe or other destinations before entering the workforce. I knew that wasn't in the realm of possibility for me at the time, but I would make that dream come true, years later.

Back to that corporate ladder and the 'road to success.' It didn't quite happen the way I had envisioned it while I was in university; I didn't get a job, work my way up said ladder to achieve CEO status as any self-respecting economics graduate would want to do. In fact, my resume was a bit of a checkerboard. It had no clear path or progression; just a hodge-podge of jobs. They included a stint as a 911 operator/ police dispatcher for Toronto Police Services; a software trainer; an administrator; a journalist; the owner of a vegan meal delivery service and marketing manager and sales rep in the high-tech industry.

The recurring theme and passion in my life has been promoting vegetarianism and veganism, fuelled by an overwhelming compassion for animals. I cry uncontrollably at the sight of slaughterhouse footage. My heart breaks when I see animals in distress or hear stories of abuse and neglect.

A turning point came after a devastating life experience in 1995, from which I eventually recovered. A key factor in the recovery process was volunteering for the Toronto Vegetarian Association (TVA), which I've now been doing for the past twelve years. I quickly learned that to get over any sort of trauma, the best thing to do is give something back to someone else.

Volunteering for a cause I believed in gave me the strength to get out of bed in the morning, when I needed it most. It helped rebuild my shattered self-esteem.

While helping out at TVA, I came to the realization that my vegetarianism was sheer hypocrisy. Not a pleasant truth to face. I learned that the egg and dairy industries are just as cruel as the beef, pork, poultry and fish industries. As if that wasn't bad enough, they're also not good for your health! Yet my resistance to change was baffling. I was a hopeless cheese-aholic; I ate ice cream by the tubful, loved yogurt and didn't think life without milk chocolate was worth living. It took a good seven months after the light bulb went on, but I finally made the leap and vowed to eliminate eggs and dairy from my diet.

This in turn gave me the courage to start my own business. *Evolving Appetites—Health Conscious Cuisine* began in 1997. It was a vegan meal delivery service aimed at providing busy, health conscious people with options outside of the usual restaurant and take-out fare; nutritious home cooked meals delivered to their door. It was a good idea—my former competitors are still doing it. However, after two years, I decided that it wasn't for me. Way too much work for not enough money and I wasn't reaching enough people with my vegan message. I wanted the 'Oprah Effect'—I wanted to reach millions!

The more urgent need, however, was money; I was tired of not having any and I hated having to think about every penny coming in. So I started fervently looking for a job. With the help of a friend, I landed a contract position as a marketing manager for a high-tech product distribution firm. Never mind that I didn't know what I was doing, or didn't have experience in high-tech marketing or distribution. During the interview, I somehow managed to convince them that hiring me was a good idea and it all worked out well. I stayed there for three and a half years, in three different positions; each progressively more challenging and of course, better paying.

That led to my job with the high-tech manufacturing company that I described earlier—territory account manager for Canada. That job became one of my most successful endeavors; if one measures success by money. I received a very respectable paycheque for running around the country (my territory was Canada), working ridiculously long hours and bearing a huge load of stress. Don't get me wrong; it was a great job and I actually loved it while I was doing it. I loved the people contact; I enjoyed giving presentations to groups of reseller sales reps who would be selling our product and I loved the travel.

But it was exhausting and really not good for my health. Eating airplane and restaurant food all the time, while breathing recycled airplane air or extremely dry hotel room air and not getting quality sleep, due to constant time changes and jet lag, is a prescription for ill health. I held up surprisingly well due to my vegan diet, but I knew that type of lifestyle was not for me long term.

At the beginning of 2005, my bank account started to look good enough for me to be able to contemplate a sabbatical and by mid-year, I knew I could pull it off. This was my dream from 22 years ago finally coming true; I was actually making it happen! I let my manager know informally and gave a written resignation in August of that year; with my last day being December 30th, 2005.

Now, all that may sound great, but it was a bit like jumping off a cliff without a parachute or knowing whether there were rocks at the bottom or a soft mattress to land on. I knew I had enough money to take all of 2006 off, but I had no clue what I would do after that. I had no job lined up, no idea of a career path and no plan. I just couldn't wait to hang up the sales rep hat and get on to the fun stuff.

The fun stuff turned out to be spending that winter at the *Ann Wigmore Health Institute* in Aguada, Puerto Rico, immersing myself in the raw and living foods lifestyle. I had a lovely apartment on the beach and got plenty of sunshine; that was truly heaven on earth. The goal was to experience what optimum health and well-being felt like. The driving force behind all that was a desire to cure or at least shrink my uterine fibroids. The theory was that eating nothing but raw plant-based foods, some of them fermented, drinking clean water, breathing clean air and virtually eliminating stress from my life would result in complete healing. Well, it did, sort of. I still have the fibroids, but the accompanying cramps and other discomfort have disappeared. A nice side effect was losing 30 lbs. I felt great!

While in Puerto Rico, I met some people who asked me to be their personal raw food chef for the summer in the Blue Ridge Mountains of North Carolina. While I only did the raw chef gig for two of the five months I was hired for, I chose to keep the lease on my apartment above a hilltop in the woods and spent an awesome summer there. I hiked, prepared my own nourishing raw/living food meals and just made taking care of myself a full-time job. I grew to love the peace and solitude. It gave me a chance to slow down and the option to think or not think.

I came home for a couple of months, before heading off to Thailand and Indonesia to avoid yet another Toronto winter. Highlights of that adventure included a one-week fasting retreat, followed by two weeks of raw foods on the island of Koh Samui, off the coast of Thailand. From there, I travelled to northern Thailand to do an 11-day silent meditation retreat just outside of Chiang Mai. I toured around various other Thai cities and towns, until it was time to head to Borneo, Indonesia to volunteer at a gibbon (primate) sanctuary. I spent two weeks at the sanctuary and about ten days in Bali, before heading back to North America.

After my sabbatical, I focused on exercising my passion of promoting veganism. I revived Evolving Appetites (www.evolvingappetites.com), but this time as a workshop and cooking class business. I reasoned that I can reach more people this way. The newly incarnated company is only a year old as I write this, but I've had moderate success. I teach vegan cooking classes at about ten different *Loblaws* cooking schools and take any and every opportunity that comes my way to present, speak or give a workshop on the topic. To fill in cash flow gaps, I take odd jobs here and there through a temp agency. This new business is very much in its infancy. So I can't really say, "I've made it" by conventional definitions of success. But as I said, my definition of success changes as I do.

I'm aiming for leaving the world a bit better by contributing to the end of cruelty to animals and the end of needless suffering by human beings who misguidedly eat these animals. I know I've made a good start by sharing my knowledge and experience through my workshops, cooking classes and other presentations. I hope to touch many others. Wish me luck.

Natascha Trivedi

My grandfather was a great businessman, known and admired by many. Sadly, he passed away before I could get to know him. My mother was eager that my sister and I should grow up knowing at least a little about the kind and gentle man whose life had touched so many others. For that reason, she would tell us stories about her own childhood. Her tales would beautifully illustrate our grandfather to us through her eyes and thanks to her, our grandfather was able to find a place in our hearts, as well.

My favourite story was one that my grandfather told my mother when she herself was a child. As the story goes, my grandfather had just arrived in the big city with nothing but a dream and a few rupees in his pocket. In the days that followed, every meal for him consisted of bread and butter, while he went knocking from door to door, trying to establish his business. Just thinking about that now, makes me realize how lucky I am to have the support behind me that he did not. I guess he was a *'solo-preneur'* in the true sense of the word.

This story was my favourite for two reasons. First, because it has a very happy ending—within a few years, my grandfather had built a strong business empire, got married and welcomed my mother into a loving and plentiful home. Secondly, the sense of 'wow' that I felt as a child has stayed with me since, as it is truly amazing to think of someone building something so substantial out of absolutely nothing.

As romantic and wonderful as it sounds to start from the bottom up, like my grandfather did, there comes a time when a reality check kicks in. Most of us feel an urge to ask the question: "What am I really doing?" If I am to be honest, I think there are a few of us who pursue university as a way to hide away from making a decision about what we really want from life. I know this because I was guilty of doing it myself. I was a good student; in fact I had so many options that I wound up being confused and frustrated.

By the time I was 18, I had won a place at one of the top universities in England (where I lived) and also at the University of Toronto, to study Political Science. For a while, I managed to convince myself that it was the right path because it seemed realistic and comparable to what those around me were doing. However soon enough, I couldn't seem to shake the nagging feeling that some part of me didn't really want that. After a turbulent few months of going back and forth, saying yes, then no, I finally made the decision not to attend university; at least not in the near future.

Making that decision was one of the hardest things that I had ever done. At the time, most of my friends were off to university and many of them thought I was crazy to turn down a 'certain future', whereby I could spend four years earning a piece of paper as assurance that I had something to offer the world. I didn't really have what could be construed as a back-up plan; my own plans seemed lofty and distant in comparison to the stability of aspiring to a regular job.

Alas, I knew that the entrepreneurial path was the one for me. I could see the big picture and the end result all too well. I could see my house, my car, my wonderful and fulfilling career and my family. In my head, I had a definite picture of what I wanted out of life and thinking about it brought me great joy; only at this point, I didn't have a clue *how* to go about it.

In the meantime, something else was happening in my life. My sister and I had fallen in love with Canada after a vacation to Toronto and we were looking to leave England to pursue our hopes and dreams afresh in this beautiful country. While deciding on how to move forward with my plans, it was a grueling wait, not knowing where I would start the pursuit of my dreams.

In 2005, we moved to Canada at just 19 and 22 years old. We had hoped to make this move with our parents, as we are a small and very close family. However, as hard as our parents have tried to make this possible, it seems that the right time for them to join us is yet to come. This has tested our courage and resolve a lot. It has been very daunting, as anyone can imagine. When I moved, I once again began to think long and hard. I thought a lot that perhaps it might be best for me to start university and for once be realistic about my future. As if a move halfway across the world wasn't stressful enough, I was still getting completely frustrated as to the 'right' path for myself. However, I realized something valuable. I came here with dreams and a vision; it is my duty to fulfill that vision—for me.

Since moving to Canada, my sister and I have co-authored one book and started two businesses; diving in heart and soul. In 2006, I got the idea to design jewelry. Always drawn to fashion, I yearned to create something that would make people feel special, while at the same time, allowing me to express myself.

The result was *Masque Mi—Designer Jewelry*. All our designs started at the drawing board and my sister and I took great pride in creating every one of them. Each piece is inspired by dramatic, colourful and artistic Venetian masks. My aim is to inspire, as well as adorn. Admittedly, this was a tricky choice for a first business as jewelry can be a tough market to break into. However, the way I see it, I'm making my own niche; not competing with anyone else for theirs.

My second and latest venture is providing assistance to small businesses and entrepreneurs. My company is called *NV Virtual Assistance* and I enjoy incorporating my passion for writing into my everyday life. Knowing first-hand how challenging it can be to have your own business, I feel I'm in the perfect position to assist others and provide support that I would have appreciated when I started out. Having learned how important it is for a business to put forth a polished image, I especially enjoy helping new businesses to put their best foot forward.

What I love about my profession is that no two days are alike. I am constantly expanding my skill-set and have the satisfaction of working with businesses from an array of different industries. I have also realized how important promotion is, no matter what the venture. A question to ask is simply, "How can you expect to succeed, if no one knows that you and your ideas exist?" It is so important to put yourself and your business 'out there'. There is nothing like building genuine and lasting relationships, but these can only be formed by taking the time and making the effort to reach out to those around you.

Don't get me wrong, sometimes it is very tempting to want to give up along the way. After a rough day, I think it's normal to feel a little down. Whenever this happens to me, I do whatever I can do to make myself feel positive again. It doesn't have to be something big, for me this can be anything from taking a walk in my favorite place in Yorkville, to listening to some music; anything that helps me unwind and bring back my inner focus. Uncertainty can be scary at first, but once I embraced my ambitions, I found myself beginning to welcome it as part of the adventure.

In my experience, it is important to be open to opportunities; even when they're sometimes hard to see. I refuse to compromise my standards and my vision and I have learnt that this path requires strength and conviction. It can be overwhelming but I strongly believe that it's easier to overcome failure and try again, than to never try.

My businesses are expanding everyday. My sister and I are also actively looking to have our book published. I am proud to say that I have come a long way in just a few short years. I have many dreams, both old and new, and some are still works in progress. I feel very lucky to have the support of my family, friends and some very inspiring mentors I have met along the way.

Had it not been for my mother and father who have always encouraged me to pursue my own dreams and continue to do so everyday, I wouldn't be on this wonderful and independent path to realizing them. I often think of the courage my grandfather had all those years ago. I also fondly think of my mother, telling me my favourite story about him before bedtime. It fills me with hope that my own story will have a happy ending too.

Karyn Chopik

I've always thought I would be a successful artist someday; I just didn't know how it would come about. As a kid, I always had my nose buried in a sketch pad or I was concocting crazy sculptures out of a variety of found objects. My interest in jewelry started in high school when my art teacher, Mr. Razenzoff, encouraged me to submit a design for the class graduation ring. I won the competition and was surprised at how easily the design came to me. I really enjoyed working with jewelry; however at the time, I didn't think I could make a living at it. My dear, practical friend, Left Brain, advised I get a profession; so I acquired a Bachelor of Education, majoring in art, at the University of Alberta. I'd intended to teach art at the high school level, but the universe had a different plan!

One day back in 1984, I was having coffee with three friends and we thought it would be fun to start making handmade jewelry. We each invested $350 and got to work. It must have been the right place and the right time; four years later, we had thirteen people working for us. We had agents across the USA and Canada and were doing almost a million dollars a year in sales. It was a magic carpet ride that seemed to have no end until the recession of the 80's hit. Consumer's taste in jewelry changed to mass-produced, lower-end products and sales dropped fast. We lost three major chain store accounts due to bankruptcy in one year. The impact was too great for our bootstrap company to survive. It wasn't long before we became insolvent and had to close our beloved company.

I decided that if you can't beat 'em, join 'em. I opened an agency in the Vancouver Show Mart, representing larger firms in the sales and distribution of mass-produced costume jewelry. Ten successful years passed, yet I longed for hands-on creativity. In 1999 I decided to follow my dreams and once again started making handmade jewelry with the birth of Karyn Chopik Studio.

My first year on my own was rather deflating for my ego. I first started Karyn Chopik Studio letting Left Brain call the shots. I created a business plan, interpreted the needs of my clients and mentored other companies that possessed that proverbial 'golden egg.' I thought I had it all figured out; I was wrong.

I committed to doing the Canadian trade show circuit. My first horse out of the shoot was the Toronto Gift Show. Left Brain told me this was one of Canada's premiere shows and it would be beneficial to be there. I talked my face off to a sea of retailers, only to come out of the show with $3500 in orders. I was devastated; after all, my background was sales. I was good at it and could write $50,000 in orders in one day with my previously owned fashion accessory agency. I wondered how on earth this could possibly be happening to me. I shared my grief with a few other established trade show participants. They told me not to take it personally. They were competitors, yet cared enough to share valuable information to support my growth. Some of us are still friends today. Whenever we see each other, we talk over dinner and discuss survival tips on how to make it as female manufacturers in a male dominated industry. It is my experience that the best advice and encouragement has come from fellow competitors. *The true nature of entrepreneurial spirit is that of cooperation. When you meet like-minded individuals, nurture that relationship.*

I continued across the country showing my wares at various tradeshows on my way back to Vancouver. Unfortunately, my negative sales experience was being repeated like a bad rap song. My financial investment was quickly being gobbled up and landing accounts was similar to giving birth; a slow and painful process. I was at a very low point in my life; my ego was bruised and my dreams appeared shattered. The success of past experience was not happening and a huge pity party was in the making!

I had other job offers in the industry and was very close to giving up. One day, I was sitting in my small studio trying to decide what to do. I already knew Left Brain's answer would be to go with the security of a regular job. I was in tears and started to pray when I felt a powerful presence. It was a strong, overwhelming sensation that made all of my hairs bristle. I felt like I was outside of my body and yet it was also happening deep within me. I was floating in a warm bath of golden light and felt a sweet, loving, female presence. Her voice was different from my own; yet it was my own voice at the same time. She told me to continue on my path.

That day, I realized that my purpose in life was to share my divine femininity through my art form. Everything in life is a test. I was driving on rocky roads, but I knew I couldn't stop believing in my dream. I spent the next few years struggling to build my business; yet the real work was being done inside. The development of my spiritual growth would bring me to a turning point; I was preparing myself for the next level.

I spent the next year exploring unknowns. I read every self-help book I could get my hands on; dove into the teachings of enlightened masters and attended wacky retreats where women beat drums and sat cross-legged on the floor until my muscles ached; all in the hopes that I could redefine my crumbled core. I realized I had a lot of baggage to shift. I studied with energy workers who gave me the tools to identify the baggage and as they would say, "spin it off." It was a time of liberation and freedom.

The great American psychic, Edward Casey, said, "Mind is the master builder." I acknowledged the fact that how I saw myself and the story I told myself was actually creating my future. It seemed as good a time as any to let go of old stories that didn't serve me and write a new script. I spent a lot of dark, lonely hours, digging deep into the abscessed part of self, yet slowly and assuredly, over time, I learned to reframe my thinking. If negative thought wasps snuck into my head, I swatted them away, clearing the room for a higher vibration to enter.

I think the turning point came in my third year. I had talked Left Brain out of doing tradeshows for a while. She had no choice; we were broke. I decided I needed someone else to do sales for me; someone who wasn't emotionally attached to my product.

Back in my days as an agent, my strongest competitor was Nan Miller Agency. She was the only person in the business who hadn't tried pirating my lines. Nan had big, powerful collections that made her buckets of money. Left Brain questioned my sanity, doubting her agency would waste their time on me; but my new healthier, intuitive side unfurled the old bandages of bruised ego and set up an appointment. Much to her staff's surprise, Nan said yes! Looking back, I asked Nan the other day, "Why did you take me on when I first came into your showroom?" She said she liked me; she knew what I was capable of and felt I had only scratched the surface of my potential. *Many important decisions are made based on gut instinct; not on what can be measured. Find people who believe in you.* Nan became my mentor, helping shape my existing collection into a more commercial product. Even though the collection wasn't making her much money, Nan didn't give up. She relentlessly continued to show the line, slowly building a customer base.

So, things were better than before, but they were still slow coming. One day, I took an honest, close look at my creations and decided I didn't really like them. I had been trying to fit into the mold and look like everyone else. The homogony was stifling me. It was the release of that next spring collection that I had a major breakthrough. I let go.

I sent Left Brain on a vacation and focused not on what the market would bear, but what I could wear! It was all about me!! If the line was a bust, at least I would have interesting jewelry to wear at my next job interview.

This was at a time when there was a downturn in the economy. Price point was everything. My new labor intensive wearable art line was high-end. There was integrity to the line that could be felt and there was nothing like it in the industry. While everyone else was doing small tailored work, my line explored bold organic shapes, oxidized mixed metals, layers of chain and my signature 'wabi sabi' styling; or the art of imperfection. Nan was a bit nervous when I showed her the new look and much higher price point, but like a trooper, she started to show it and it was a hit! As *William Shakespeare's Polonius* said, "To thine own self be true." The same was true for my process as a designer. I had done some much needed work on me and had come to the conclusion that it is my truth or personal vibration that must be expressed. It is my vibration that others of like mind are attracted to, not an illusion of someone else's reality. They say only 5% of the population are capable of original thought; the rest are copy cats. *Original thought comes from knowing who you are; not being afraid to expose yourself and take risks.*

By the fourth year of Karyn Chopik Studio, things were really happening for me. I was getting into key accounts and developing a loyal following. I realized it was now timely to start branding my name. I interviewed some graphic design houses that had a reputation in the industry, but it felt like wading through mud, trying to explain to them the image I was striving for. One day, a friend recommended a young multi-media artist by the name of Todd Higden. She trained his dog in obedience and she said she just knew he was the one. How crazy is that! *The best recommendations are word of mouth and they are always surrounded by a hunch.*

Todd was a tall, dark and handsome man originally from Montreal. As soon as we met, I knew he got what I was about. There was synchronicity; something that can't be bought based on others' past performances. Synchronicity is felt deep inside. It is an 'aha' moment where you say to yourself, 'I have known this person before. There is a sweet note of familiarity being with them.' Todd is now like a brother to me. When we work together on a project, there is an incredible creative buzz between us and we are like two drunken teenagers, giddy with delight. He believed in my vision. He redesigned my logo and company image; transforming an artisan line to one of international appeal. He created an amazing website, table top posters and postcards for the retailer's point of display and the most important feature of all- my bio card.

At first, I was reluctant to have a bio card. I worried it might be egotistical. I will never forget showing the rough draft to a woman whose opinion I respected. She mirrored my fears saying that it was pretentious. She said people are interested in my jewelry - not me. I almost bought into it, but my new and improved inner voice told me to press forward. The bio card was one of the best things I ever did.

It became an exercise in breaking through old beliefs that I wasn't worthy. Now, every piece of jewelry purchased comes with one. The consumer keeps it and shares it with her friends. Sales exploded after the bio cards were introduced. I put myself out there and the universe responded in kind.

I read somewhere that if someone sees your name three times, they remember you. Well, all the branding must have paid off because people were now recognizing my jewelry on other women at cocktail parties and in the boardroom. It was like a secret society of women, looking deep into each other's souls through the medium of jewelry; or as left brain would put it, a great conversational ice breaker!

Speaking of left brain-yikes, I'd sent her on a holiday! I now needed her desperately to return. This was a time of great change. Karyn Chopik Studio Ltd was a separate entity from me and had a life force of its own. Things were happening so fast that I was scrambling to keep up. The business had exploded, production schedules were at capacity and I was hiring workers left, right and centre to keep up with the demand for my jewelry.

Up until that point, I had been managing everything on my own, but things soon hit critical mass. I was exhausted, trying to balance a home life and career. My workday started at 6:00 am and ended at 9:00 pm. Like an alcoholic, I would sneak away and work during times when I was supposed to be socializing. I was burning out fast.

One day, a friend advised me that I was heading for a heart attack if I didn't hire someone to help with operations. Her words, albeit a bit extreme, struck a note with me. I realized the business had outgrown my capacity. I had to release any proprietary possessiveness and bring in the big guns. *Entrepreneurs are hands-on. The hardest lesson for a mid-sized business is giving up control and learning to trust.*

I put my company's finances into other, more capable hands; I hired a production manager to implement systems and coordinate the constant flow of orders. Even the creative process changed. I was now working with a design team, planning the line and marketing campaign six months in advance of its release. I still worked around the clock as the business morphed in new directions, but at least I knew that if I could actually pull it off, things would be better. Many times that niggling negative voice in my head told me I wasn't smart enough, but then Warrior Woman kicked into gear. My Rambo Girl in face paint and camo clothing plowed through the walls of fear and resistance. I was in a rubber raft surging down the rapids and the only thing I could do was hold on for dear life and wait for calmer waters.

During the next couple of years, a really lovely thing happened. Karyn Chopik Studio Ltd reached calmer waters. All our hard work paid off. We now had systems in place and I had a chance to walk amongst the living again. We revisited doing USA and Canadian trade shows, but this time with our eye on a long range goal of establishing a strong footprint in the marketplace.

This was also a time of many fortunate blessings. *Lady luck is a sexy old bird; just when you think she has forgotten you, she blows you a kiss.* Lucky breaks came my way when I least expected them and from unsolicited sources. For example, my friend, Raeanne, unknowingly showed her friend, Taffi Rosen, her latest photo shoot; which happened to be of my jewelry. Taffi loved my work and included me in her TV series, *"In the Mind Of"* shown on *Biography Channel* (*Brava* in the USA).

Another example came when I did a trunk show at a store in Victoria, where I met a woman from Toronto, named Bianca Bartz. I felt an instant connection with Bianca, who was in Victoria visiting her mother when they wandered into the trunk show. She turned out to be the editor of the largest trend spotting website in the world. Their features reach an audience of over 1,000,000 people a day and are often picked up by the New York Times. She responded to my jewelry and wrote a wonderful article.

As a result, Karyn Chopik Studio was now being featured on websites around the world. My exposure had increased a gazillion fold all because of that serendipitous encounter. Old Lefty would say that we have paid our dues and are now being rewarded, but the artist in me prefers to see it as a matching of vibrations where the colors just seem to blend.

Right now, I can't really say where my company is headed. Left

Brain has us on a five-year plan with quarterly projections and cash flow charts. Truthfully, I think my jewelry is organic, so it would seem that my journey is also an organic process. My inner work has paid off as I am not attached to outcomes. I free fall a lot. At times, it feels like I'm jumping from a plane without a parachute, but then another westward wind carries me to the next destination. One thing I do know; someday I'm going to be a successful artist. That is for sure!

Looking back, I would like to acknowledge some wonderful beings who have aided me on my journey. I am blessed to have you all in my life. Thank you to my dear friend, Raeanne Holoboff for always being there. You have selflessly photographed my jewelry since day one and you have done it because you believe in me. To my companion and polar opposite Keltie Lang: Thank you for always encouraging me to see the other side. Thank you for helping me understand computers, Photoshop, Simply Accounting, and everything else that is technical. Sorry, but I still need more work learning how to program the VCR! Big hugs go to my best friend and sister, Kathy Chopik. You are the smartest left Brain I know! Biscuits and pats to my golden retriever, The Little Prince of Shoreland. Thank you for showing me what unconditional love feels like. I send heartfelt gratitude to my co-workers, both past and present: Elizabeth, Jacquie, Tracey, Susan, Debra, Lise, Raffaella, Janelle, Kathy, Colleen and Danel. Thank you for helping me build Karyn Chopik Studio. To my fabulous agent and friend, Nan Miller; you are the best!

Roula Papaioannou

In November 2008, I was talking to a friend on the phone when I suddenly said to her, "I love my job, but there is something coming for me that will cause me to leave my job early in 2009." She laughed and asked me how I could possibly know that. I said, "Something inside me just tells me it's so." As I said that, my body felt at ease and my mind felt peace, as well. That was Clarity. Clarity is a gift I have come to appreciate a great deal. I realized this gift called Clarity could also be the result of getting older and beginning to trust my instincts a lot more. I understood that all experiences were necessary on my path to realizing my true potential.

On Christmas Day of that year, one of my oldest and best friends gave me a gift that would prove to change my life in a great way. That great book, called *Ecoholic*, outlined effective methods to living a greener life on Canadian soil. My friend had been trying to get me interested in the concept for at least two years; but in the past, I hadn't been open to such change. Although the world around me at that point was screaming for people of all ages to wake up and take a stand to protect our environment, I had been so set in my ways that I had completely ignored the screams. At the age of 26, I worked for the largest cosmetic company in the world. I specifically was working with a skin care brand with a dermatological background. With this brand, I was responsible for training those working within major pharmacies all across Canada. Did I love my job? Absolutely! I was all about travelling and meeting people and public speaking had become a newfound passion of mine. The job had allowed me to gain confidence in ways I had never previously imagined. Not only that, I had had the opportunity to see all of Canada and work with the most amazing people on this planet.

My love for skincare didn't start with my job. It began in my teen years; I remember saving my allowance to buy a *Biotherm* moisturizer at the young age of 14. I have to admit to being somewhat obsessed with keeping my skin healthy. My friend, who I had known since kindergarten, was determined to challenge my one track mind when it came to my skin care knowledge.

So, on that Christmas Day, I unwrapped the book and thought, "Here she goes again; trying to get me to go green." That time was different, though, because the book caught my eye. I asked myself if there was something working there; was there a message in all of it? Was I supposed to use my passion for skincare for something other than the brand I had been working with for the last three years? If you were to ask anybody who knew me, they would call me the voice of the brand. Everyone knew that the brand I was working for was where I was at my best.

The next day would prove that bad habits were hard to break. I had never read a book chapter by chapter; I tended to skip to the chapters that were of particular relevance to me. There was a chapter in the new book that focused on green alternatives to skincare. I was always drawn to issues on skincare, so it was no surprise that I automatically launched into that part of the book. As I sat there reading, I found myself asking questions of the beauty world that had never occurred to me before. Were cosmetic companies producing products that contain ingredients also used to create anti-freeze? Could it be possible that the ingredients some companies used were also well known carcinogens? How could that be? I became determined to finally take a stand. As uncomfortable as that made me, I knew I had to do it. I felt like I had been wearing blinders and it was time to take the blinders off. "Yikes," I thought, "what if all of this is true..." I couldn't put the book down; it was fascinating. I felt like I was back in school, where I was taught to push the envelope. As I read on, I noticed that a specific skin care company was being mentioned more than others. I saw that this particular brand was mentioned over a dozen times as being safe for the environment. *Burt's Bees* was rated highly because of their natural approach to skincare. I was fascinated; I had always known *Burt's Bees* to produce a great lip product, but never thought to look further. As my curiosity grew, I went online and Googled the brand. I read all about their natural and safe approach to skincare. I immediately decided that I wanted to work for this company and change the world. What if I could do what I had been doing for my current brand; which was creating excitement, but for a brand that could prove to alter the future lives of the kids I wanted to have ? Not thinking too much about it, I wrote a cover letter and resume and addressed it to their home office in North Carolina, stating:

"Dear Burt's Bees,
This is a formal letter stating my interest in working with your brand as a National Training Manager for Canada."

There had been no posting for the job; I simply asked for what I wanted.

The New Year came in quietly and I still couldn't shake the feeling that the job I had and loved would soon be changing. I remember my sister always being envious of my job because I would often work from home when I wasn't travelling. She considered this to be a cushy job; she thought my job was easy. She kept alluding to the fact that I had the easiest job in the world. Normally, my response would have been some sort of retort, indicating to her that my job seemed easy because I didn't show anxiety as much as I felt it. You can imagine, there is some level of anxiety when travelling, living out of a suitcase and speaking to groups of up to 300 people. When, in the first week of January, my sister once again commented, "Boy, if I had your job, I would be so relaxed; you have it good." my response was different. With complete confidence, I replied:

"So Niki, you know how you think my job is easy? Watch what comes next: I will have a great leader that will inspire me to grow; a team of people, one warmer than the next; I will still work from home; I will make more money and have less stress than I have now. My boss will love animals; I will still travel and inspire change; I will love the job even more and the next one will be one that will change me for the better. My boss at some point will think of me as an angel and she will be gentle in her approach that will teach me to live a better life ."

Niki laughed and said, "Roula, any more relaxed and you will be sleeping standing up." I laughed and with a great deal of clarity said, "You watch and you will see." She really didn't believe that anything like that would happen.

On February 4, 2009, I was surfing a job search website on the internet when I come across a posting headed, "National Training Manager for Canada with *Burt's Bees*." I almost fell off of my chair as I wondered if they ever got the resume that I had sent right after Christmas. The posting was perfect and applications were to be made through the website.

I never take the normal route to anything. It's in my Aquarius nature to be different. So, instead of applying through the website, I did a Google search for *Burt's Bees* in the media. It was clear to me that here was the position I wanted; all I needed was to send my resume to the person who would be managing me in the future. I found *Burt's Bees* mentioned in the *National Post*, with a quote from the Marketing Manager. I quickly jotted down her name and figured out what her email address would be. I updated the resume I had sent to the North Carolina office in late 2008 and emailed it to the Marketing Manager mentioned in the article. I knew that it was what I had to do and if something was going to come of it; it would be a real shot.

Forty-eight hours later, that I had received a response from *Burt's Bees'* Marketing Manager herself. She let me know that she would be interested in meeting with me. I immediately called her and she responded, "Roula, we were so happy to receive your resume. It was like an angel placed it on my desk." I felt great as she said this and we arranged an interview.

Ultimately, I had three interviews; back to back. I had been fighting a fever, but I felt that the interviews had gone well, in spite of my body heating up. I left the interviews with a sense of accomplishment and a small dose of guilt. I felt like I was cheating on my current employer, the cosmetic giant. I went home that night to deal with flu. I had always believed in the mind-body connection, so my illness may have been the guilt that I felt about going to an interview with another company.

After two days of being sick, I decided to get up and check my email. There it was; *Burt's Bees* wanted me to interview for a fourth time by having me do a ten-minute presentation to company employees on a particular line of products they had assigned. I was happy and stressed. I had to take ten slides and make a ten-minute presentation to people who may become my future manager and her team. My job kept me busy, but that interview was at the top of my mind as I tried to get through that week.

The big day finally arrived and I walked into the corporate offices of *Burt's Bees* all smiles and sweaty palms. I was greeted by a very professional woman who turned out to be the Marketing Manager. She led me into the room I would be presenting in and offered me a glass of water. I was impressed; a glass of water, not a bottle, recycling bins all over the place, with the lights off and blinds open to get the natural light. I was registering all of the elements as I set up my equipment. About 15 minutes later, twenty people sat in front of me and waited for my show to begin. The presentation that was to be ten minutes in length grew into thirty amazing minutes.

I was received very well, surprised to be asked to leave the room for a moment when I finished. I was expecting feedback and criticism and comments on how I could improve at that point in the proceedings. I was graciously led from the room and given a tour of the office. I was fairly confused at this point, wondering what was coming next.

Eventually, I was led back into the presentation room, where the General Manager presented me with a job offer on the spot. I was stunned at the speed with which it had all occurred.

Remember the list I had given my sister of my future job qualities? There it was on a sheet of paper, right in front of me. My new job would give me more freedom, a great title, an amazing salary, great benefits, the freedom to work from home and the road, a car allowance for a car of my choice and the opportunity to work with warmest group of people I had ever met.

To end my story, I'll finish by saying I accepted the offer, gave the cosmetic giant 6 weeks' notice and left to be the National Training Manager for *Burt's Bees Canada* to spread the news that a natural approach to skincare is the answer. The lesson here for me is to always trust the process of life. Some additional lessons are: accept what is given to you and know that you can always handle it, because we are never given something we cannot handle; love your job, be passionate about something and go for it; do what you love so that it never feels like a job; get creative and lastly, ask for what you want, know that it is possible and go out and get it.

I know this job will allow me to make a huge contribution to society and the environment. I will make a change in this world through helping customers realize the dangers that lie in traditional cosmetic formulas. I will show that *Burt's Bees* is not only a brand that sells and produces the most natural skincare formulas; but one that respects the earth on a grand scale. Who knows; maybe one day my message will go international. For now, I will perfect the message for *Burt's Bees* nationally and love every part of my job.

A special tribute must go to my friend, Marian Raty, and her late father, Mr. Perrti Raty. He was a man that lived his life always aware of those around him; always helping those in need. He may have left this earth a little earlier than we would have hoped, but he leaves behind a daughter who is committed to changing this earth. Marian, thank you for the book and thank you for the push; you are the reason that I am here today. I will love you always,

Roula Papaioannou